TONIA BUXTON
THE SECRET OF
SPICE

Recipes and ideas to help you live longer, look younger and feel your very best

For my family: Paul, Antigoni, Sophia, Zephyros & Zeno. All very vocal food critics with spicy palates who drive me nuts and whom I love and adore.

Published by Lagom
An imprint of Bonnier Books UK
3.08, The Plaza,
535 Kings Road,
Chelsea Harbour,
London SW10 0SZ

www.bonnierbooks.co.uk

Hardback 978-1788701075
eBook 978-1788701082

A CIP catalogue of this book is available from the British Library.

Project editor: Carly Cook
Design and art direction: HART STUDIO
Food stylist: Jaswinder Jhalli
Props stylist: Hannah Wilkinson

Printed and bound in Spain

1 3 5 7 9 10 8 6 4 2

CONTENTS

INTRODUCTION

They say variety is the spice of life – and this book is definitely testament to that.

I will show you how integral spice is to our diet, and how it can improve every aspect of our physical and mental health. Life can be overwhelming: we are all too busy, too tired or too stressed, often wishing we could lose that stubborn half a stone or get that extra hour's sleep at night.

We demand so much from our diet: we are desperate for food that is easy and quick to make but tastes delicious and that does us more good than the vitamins we are too busy to take. Recipes, it seems, have to work harder than ever. But what if I told you that by adding some cinnamon or turmeric to your food you could lose those extra pounds, or that rosemary would help you look that bit younger? How about that fennel and nutmeg would help settle your hormones, that aniseed would help you get your much-coveted eight hours sleep a night, or that ginger would help you feel sexier?

With over 50 delicious recipes inspired by the food I serve my family, this book will show how adding a little spice to everyday dishes can have a huge impact on every area of your life.

The eight key conditions I will be focusing on are: weight loss, ageing, fertility, hormone balance, mood food, libido, sleep and fatigue, and stress and migraine.

I promise you, a pinch of the right spice will alter the way you look and feel for the better – and for good.

CONDITIONS AND SPICES USED

The conditions and spices I will focus on are:

AGEING:

Basil + Cinnamon + Coriander + Garlic + Oregano + Rosemary + Sage + Thyme + Turmeric

LIBIDO:

Aniseed + Basil + Clove + Cumin + Garlic + Ginger + Nutmeg + Parsley + Saffron

MOOD FOOD:

Cacao + Chilli + Cinnamon + Nutmeg + Saffron + Sage + Turmeric

HORMONE STABILITY:

Basil + Chilli + Cumin + Fennel + Garlic + Nutmeg + Turmeric

FERTILITY:

Aniseed + Chilli + Cinnamon + Clove + Cumin + Fennel + Saffron + Sage + Thyme + Turmeric

INSOMNIA AND FATIGUE:

Aniseed + Basil + Cardamom + Chilli + Cumin + Fennel + Mint + Nutmeg + Parsley + Saffron + Sumac

STRESS AND MIGRAINE:

Basil + Cacao + Cardamom + Clove + Cumin + Nutmeg + Oregano + Rosemary + Saffron + Sage + Thyme

WEIGHT LOSS:

Chilli + Cinnamon + Cumin + Garlic + Sumac + Turmeric

HOW TO LOOK YOUNGER, BE MORE FERTILE, HEALTHIER AND HAPPIER USING SPICES

Once I hit 50, I kept being asked what creams I was applying or what supplements I was taking, as I looked younger than my age and had lots of energy. When I thought about it, it seemed to me that it was all lifestyle-based. I have always worn an SPF (mainly because after having children my skin pigments in the sun), which has definitely helped my skin, but the main thing is what I eat. Being Greek, it was easy for me to follow the colourful Mediterranean diet of my ancestors, by which I mean my grandparents.

I also felt the need to override the genes that had been passed down to me; both my parents have high blood pressure and varicose veins, have had both their knees replaced, and are on cholesterol medication. One is also a Type 2 diabetic.

I qualified as a nutritionist in my mid-twenties, but so much was so wrong with the thinking back then. I alas went through the high carb and low-fat fad, which did substantial damage to my body. So then I then started to do my own research and went back to my Greek Cypriot roots. I started eating a colourful diet of plant-based seasonal food, with lots of pulses, good fats, carbohydrates and protein, but the main ingredient in my diet was LOTS of herbs and spices. I have never in the last 30 years cooked a meal without at least two or three herbs and spices. I did this originally because it makes the food taste so much better, but continue to do so as the spices were clearly beneficial to my own and my family's health.

If you are trying to get yourself or your partner in the mood, try making food with parsley and sage, which contains Coenzyme Q10 and zinc, known for increasing libido. If you are trying to burn a little fat, then add some chilli to everything you eat – it has been proved to raise your metabolism. And if you are desperate for some sleep and would like to de-stress, then just baking a soothing chamomile cupcake and drinking a turmeric latte will make you feel so much better.

You can use this book as a simple cookbook that's full of delicious, tasty recipes, but I think the food tastes even better when you understand how all the spices are improving your health.

Spices have been used to heal since the beginning of time. The healers and witches of old knew how powerful they are, but modern living has made us forget, so I want to re-educate people about their power.

Many spices and herbs used are unusual and may be better taken in capsule form, but most can easily be incorporated into your daily cooking, so not only will your food be more interesting, but you will be making yourself well and future-proofing your health, too.

Turmeric is currently the spice of the moment. I have quite literally been screaming about its benefits for years now! However, because it is fairly cheap, the big pharmaceutical companies did not want us to know about how amazing it can be! I predict the next two rock star spices will be cumin and cinnamon.

Cumin may be helpful for people trying to lose weight. A study involving overweight adults compared the effects of cumin with a weight-loss medication and a placebo. After eight weeks, the researchers found that the cumin and weight-loss medication groups both lost significant amounts of weight, while people in the cumin group also experienced a decrease in their insulin levels. Another study found that overweight and obese women who consumed three grams of ground cumin in yogurt daily for three months had significant decreases in body weight, waist size and body fat.

Study after study shows the benefits of herbs and spices. One study at Malmö University Hospital in Sweden showed that up to two hours after eating, people who ate cinnamon-spiced rice pudding had significantly lower blood glucose levels than those who had eaten the unspiced version. Other studies suggest that cinnamon may improve blood glucose levels by increasing a person's insulin sensitivity. A 2003 trial of 60 people with Type 2 diabetes reported that consuming as little as two teaspoons of cinnamon daily for six weeks reduced blood glucose levels significantly. It also improved blood cholesterol and triglyceride levels, perhaps because insulin plays a key role in regulating fats in the body.

I have chosen my top spices and herbs, but there are many more you can use. They are full of micronutrients and you can only benefit from using them! I hope this book is an introduction to adding more spices into your diet.

AN INTRODUCTION TO KYPS

'How many psychologists does it take to change a lightbulb? One, but the lightbulb has got to want to change! OK, so it's the world's worst joke, but it's a pretty clear message. Nothing in your life is going to change by reading this book, unless you let it. You will not get healthier, stronger or happier by simply looking through the pages (well, maybe happier!). You may pick up some fun facts and perhaps even cook some amazing food, but if you really want to get the best out of this book, then decide here and now, that this book is going to change things in your life for the better, starting right now!' – Kyprianos Constantinou (Kyps)

Kyprianos Constantinou BSc MSc MBPsS graduated from Aston University with a Master's degree in Health Psychology. He first obtained a Bachelors degree in Human Psychology, which was accredited by the British Psychological Society (BPS), where his grade qualified him for graduate membership of the society.

As a student of Health Psychology, Kyps has had a particular focus on nutrition, physical activity, ageing, stress management, business psychology, smoking/drinking cessation and disease management. By using his knowledge of human behaviour and models of behavioural change, he has a firm understanding of how to increase the success rate of behavioural interventions. Kyps often works with businesses in enhancing work-related behaviours by changing work culture, while reducing stress levels and promoting healthy work perspectives. Furthermore, he has a particular interest in the effects of food and nutrition on the brain and how they manipulate our behaviour. This interest has allowed him to understand how to achieve desired behavioural effects through nutrition and diet.

According to Kyps, being healthy is not about living longer, but about living *stronger* to get the most out of your life, regardless of its duration. He believes that everybody has their own personal maximum health potential, which can be achieved through healthy living. Although the goal is not to be perfect, his aim is to get people as close to their health potential as possible, so that they can get the most out of their lives. By changing just a few aspects of life and diet, Kyps believes that people can greatly reduce their risk of disease and maintain a healthy life balance, but as is true with most things, he is adamant that you must want to make the change for yourself. He specialises in helping people understand why they should want to make those changes.

In his work, Kyps is often asked to deliver presentations and seminars to businesses, in order to promote healthy mental attitudes. Some of the subjects Kyps has presented on include stress mastery, increasing physical activity in the workplace, helping women take control of their lives at home and with their career, changing workplace culture from the bottom up and the top down, and how we can build our future bodies and minds using nothing but nutrition and positive mental attitude. Although these issues relate to different aspects of behaviour, Kyps excels at identifying why we need to change behaviours, how to make the changes in the least disruptive and most effective way possible and what to do if we relapse. He enjoys writing about behavioural change and has produced works in which he explains how people can take control of their own behaviours, with higher chances of success and lower rates of relapse. He also worked with me on *Eat Greek For A Week*, where food was used as a way to enhance health and achieve specific behavioural effects.

Kyps has used his expertise to work closely with me on this book identifying the ways in which my recipes can improve our health and wellbeing, while reducing the risks and symptoms of various ailments in the body and mind. Though the focus is on eight different aspects of health, by exploring each spice individually you will also discover the various other ways in which these herbs and spices can enhance your life and why they have been used to promote health for thousands of years.

There couldn't be a tastier way to change your life. Simply read the recipes, use the spices and cook the mouth-watering meals to experience the wide range of health benefits, while learning all about how these spices made their way into our kitchen to begin with. Explore the history and mythology of each spice while understanding how they enhance your mind and your body, and get lost in a world of mystery and aroma.

SPICE
FOR LIFE

Living a long, healthy and fulfilled life is pretty much at the top of
everyone's wish list. Looking good, feeling great and having enough
energy to get through the day are all directly linked to how we fuel our
bodies. It's all very well having a classically healthy diet, but mixing
good food with specific spices can make all the difference
and leave you brimming with energy and radiance.
It definitely helps to slow down the hands
of time when it comes to ageing.

AGEING AND SLOWING IT DOWN

For me, combatting ageing is not just about looking good, it's about feeling good too, which is down to two things: energy and attitude. A few years ago I caught myself making old lady noises every time I got up or sat down and it made me determined not to get into lazy habits. Being youthful is a state of mind and it's certainly something that we should embrace wholeheartedly – it's never too late.

The first thing you learn when you study the psychology of ageing is that nobody ever looked at their watch and thought 'oh, there it is, time to go' and then died. Since the beginning of time, nobody has actually died of old age. If we have eaten nutritious foods and lived a healthy lifestyle, it is highly unlikely that we will age in the same way as the junk food kings of our generation. The message is that it is never too early to start, or too late to make the change. If we are lucky enough to reach old age, let's make sure we can own it when we get there and stay as healthy and active as possible.

With modern medicine and technology, one thing that is certain is that we are living longer. However, the sad thing is, we are not always living stronger. For all the medication that is out there, nothing can increase quality of life in your twilight years more than the quality of the food you eat in your earlier in life. Medication can keep us alive for longer, but there is NO medication that can reverse the effects of a lifetime of unhealthy choices.

One thing we can do is recognise that all the cells in our bodies are made up of three things: the air we breathe, the liquids we drink and the food we consume. Since we were in the womb, every hair on our heads, every skin follicle or muscle strand in our body, every blood cell and internal organ has been created from what we have put into our bodies. Yes, there are elements of genetics involved, but ultimately, nothing in your body will reach its genetic potential without the best nutrition, and you will simply end up as a lesser version of your true potential. Take a second to stop and think about your consumption of food and drink over your lifetime. Think about everything you've eaten that has become part of you, and you will start to get a picture of your body. Remember, you cannot rewind the clock or start again. What you can do though, is make a change right now and start feeding your body for the future version of yourself.

ESSENTIAL VITAMINS AND MINERALS

VITAMIN A is great for anyone wishing to reduce the signs of ageing in their face. The nutrients in this vitamin have the ability to reduce the dark circles that appear around our eyes as we age, by strengthening the skin to keep it tighter as it gets heavier. Vitamin A deficiency is often linked to scaly skin and it can also reduce the body's natural lubrication of the skin. This vitamin is also highly beneficial to hair health as it promotes natural oils, which keeps your hair and scalp healthy and can also slow down hair loss. Foods rich in this vitamin include carrots, winter squash, cantaloupe melon, apricots, spinach, kale and spring greens.

VITAMIN B3 is important for keeping the skin moist and vitamin B6 is essential for the creation of haemoglobin, which transports oxygen around the body to our muscles, organs and cells. The richest sources of vitamin B3 are poultry, salmon, tuna, liver, peas, peanuts, mushrooms and sunflower seeds, while vitamin B6 is found in pork, poultry, fish, bread, wholegrain cereals, such as brown rice and oatmeal, soya beans, peanuts, potatoes and eggs.

VITAMIN C is a natural antioxidant, which can destroy free radicals that can cause oxidative stress and damage to our cells and have even been known to cause cancers. Vitamin C is also known to strengthen the immune system, which also protects the skin from the sun and helps collagen production. Excellent sources of this vitamin include citrus fruit, cantaloupe melon, mango, papaya, strawberries, broccoli, spinach and other leafy greens, tomatoes and winter squash.

VITAMIN D deficiency has been known to cause brittle bones and weak muscles as we age. There is also the risk of certain cancers developing when vitamin D levels are low. Make sure you regularly consume this vitamin, as it will aid in the development of cells, bone, hair and skin, keeping you looking and feeling younger. Excellent sources include tuna, mackerel, salmon, beef, cheese, egg yolks and food fortified with vitamin D, such as plant-based milks and cereals.

VITAMIN E is essential for healthy ageing. The effects of this vitamin are plentiful and include lowering the risk of heart disease and some cancers. Vitamin E has also been known to protect cell membrane transportation, which can stop harmful substances getting into our cells. It can also reduce inflammation in the joints and muscles and can protect the health of our eyes. Research has also identified this as a vitamin that can reduce the risk of dementia. Good sources include sunflower seeds, almonds, hazelnuts and avocado.

VITAMIN K has also been found to reduce dark circles around the eyes by stopping the leaking of capillaries, which cause dark circles and the reddening of the skin. Vitamin K can also improve the health of our bones as we age. Excellent sources of this vitamin include avocado, kale, Swiss chard, spinach, broccoli, Brussels sprouts, chicken, beef liver, pork chops, green beans and kiwi fruit.

IRON is important for keeping us active as deficiency of it leads to anaemia, which can cause fatigue. It is also responsible for the transportation of blood around the body, which is how we get our energy. Rich sources of iron include shellfish, spinach, liver and other offal, legumes, red meat, pumpkin seeds, quinoa, turkey and broccoli.

MAGNESIUM is important for the maintenance of muscle and nerve health, both of which would otherwise decrease over time. Magnesium is found in dark chocolate, avocado, nuts, legumes, tofu, seeds, salmon, wholegrains, mackerel and bananas.

ZINC is important for healthy hair and a healthy scalp. It is also beneficial for those who are trying to incorporate vitamin A into their diets, as it increases the amount of the vitamin in the blood. Wounds may also repair faster, as zinc helps tissue regeneration. Rich sources of zinc include red meat, shellfish, seeds, cashew nuts, pine nuts, almonds, dairy, dark chocolate and wholegrains.

RECOMMENDED HERBS AND SPICES

ALLSPICE	CHILLI	GARLIC	ROSEMARY
ANISEED	CINNAMON	GINGER	SAFFRON
BASIL	CLOVE	MINT	SAGE
BLACK PEPPER	CORIANDER	NUTMEG	SUMAC
CACAO	CUMIN	OREGANO	THYME
CARDAMOM	FENNEL	PARSLEY	TURMERIC

CORIANDER

(CORIANDRUM SATIVUM)

IT MIGHT ONLY BE A SMALL GREEN PLANT BEST KNOWN
FOR SPICING UP YOUR CURRIES OR SALSA, BUT
DON'T UNDERESTIMATE CORIANDER'S
ABILITY TO KEEP YOU WRINKLE
AND BLEMISH-FREE.

ORIGIN OF THE SPICE AND HISTORY

The exact origin of coriander is not known, though evidence suggests that the plant is native to Southern Europe, North Africa and Southwest Asia. The oldest evidence of coriander was discovered in a cave in Israel, from around 6000 BC. Several historical texts and documents have mentioned coriander over the ages. An ancient Sanskrit text suggests that coriander was grown in the gardens of ancient India about 7,000 years ago.

Coriander made its way to Britain via the Romans around the first century AD – they were known to flavour their breads with coriander, but some of its earliest use in Britain was as a preservative, particularly when combined with vinegar and cumin.

Though coriander was originally used as an aphrodisiac or to reduce flatulence, in modern times its curative use is limited to making modern medicines more palatable. The seeds are used as flavour enhancers in various foods, such as sausages, pastries and curries, and the leaves are commonplace in Latin American, Chinese and Indian cuisine.

FOLKLORE

It is rumoured that the name coriander came from the Greek word 'koris' which translates as 'stink bug'. It has been suggested that the name originated from the scent given off when the leaves of the plant are damaged.

In Ayurvedic medicine, coriander is said to be beneficial for all body types, which is known as 'tridoshic' in Ayurvedic terminology.

Coriander was used as a medicine, and particularly as an aphrodisiac, for centuries in Europe during the Middle Ages, where it was commonly added to love potions.

Coriander was also used in Britain by gin distillers and is to this day one of the main botanical components of gin.

HOLISTIC BENEFITS OF CORIANDER

Several things in coriander make it an effective digestive aid and it can reduce the symptoms of constipation, diarrhoea, nausea and vomiting. By promoting the secretion of digestive enzymes, coriander has also been known to treat abdominal colic.

Studies have shown that coriander can **reduce blood pressure** in those suffering from hypertension. The calcium in it aids the blood by reducing tension and this, in turn, reduces the risk of stroke and heart failure. Regular consumption of coriander contributes to the fight against heart diseases as the herb contains nutrients that can help lower the build-up of harmful cholesterol in the inner walls of the veins and arteries, which would otherwise cause stroke and atherosclerosis. It also raises the level of good cholesterol in the blood, which is effective for the prevention of other diseases.

Coriander can also **regulate sugar absorption** and reduce sugar levels in the blood, which makes it effective in the battle against diabetes. By increasing insulin secretion, it can also protect those suffering with diabetes by reducing the risk of blood sugar spikes.

Coriander has been known to **improve bone health**. Several minerals found in it, including calcium, are essential for the prevention of bone deterioration and aid in the durability of bones. This is essential for prevention of diseases such as osteoporosis and bone atrophy that are caused by malnourished bones.

The iron in coriander aids in the prevention and treatment of **anaemia**. Daily consumption of iron is essential for avoiding fatigue and maintaining healthy energy levels.

The antioxidant and antifungal properties of coriander make it valuable for healthy ageing. Not only do these components help in the maintenance of healthy and strong skin, but the vitamins and minerals found in coriander (particularly vitamin A) promote good eye health and reduce the risk of eye diseases such as macular degeneration.

NUTRITIONAL VALUE

Coriander contains vitamins A, C and K. There are also some B-complex vitamins in it including B1, B2, B3, B5, B6 and B9, as well as calcium, iron, magnesium, manganese and potassium.

ROSEMARY

························

(ROSMARINUS OFFICINALIS)

THIS IS ONE OF THE MOST AROMATIC HERBS.
WHILE IT IS OFTEN PAIRED WITH ROAST LAMB
AND GARLIC, IT IS ALSO KNOWN FOR ITS
ANTI-AGEING QUALITIES AND HAS BEEN
CALLED 'THE HERB OF YOUTH'.

ORIGIN OF THE SPICE AND HISTORY

Rosemary is native to the Mediterranean and some parts of Asia. It has been used as a natural medicine for thousands of years, and was sacred to the ancient Egyptians who had various uses for it, including embalming. The ancient Greeks and Romans also held the herb in the highest regard.

Used as a natural memory enhancer, rosemary became popular among scholars and researchers. Pliny, a famous Roman author, was one of the first to report its memory-enhancing abilities. The ancient Greeks are thought to have worn rosemary in their hair when studying for an exam because of its memory-boosting capabilities.

Nicholas Culpeper's *Complete Herbal*, the first British herbal book, was published in the sixteenth century, and mentioned the various benefits of rosemary, including its use as an elixir of youth. The author also described this wonderful herb's ability to cast out ill health from one's body.

Today, people still grow rosemary in their gardens, where it is a form of natural pest control. Its scent is still popular in cosmetics, perfumes and aromatherapy. In the kitchen, rosemary's uses include flavouring meats, soups, sauces and as a seasoning on vegetables.

FOLKLORE

The name rosemary is said to be derived from the Latin translation of '*rosmarinus*', meaning 'dew of the sea'. This may be due to the fact that it was first discovered growing by the sea.

The Virgin Mary has been linked with rosemary in stories of the Holy Family's escape to Egypt – it was said that Mary slept under a rosemary bush while her blue cloak dried on its leaves. When she took back her cloak, the white flowers of the plant had miraculously turned blue.

In ancient times, it was thought that rosemary would only grow in the gardens of the righteous, where it would protect the virtuous folk from evil. For this reason, it became popular for Greeks and Romans to grow rosemary bushes in their gardens.

Thought to be a memory aid, people placed rosemary in their pillows in order to enhance their memory and retain the day's information.

HOLISTIC BENEFITS OF ROSEMARY

The list of health benefits of this herb is vast, so here are just a few. For over a thousand years, rosemary has been thought to enhance cognition. Recent studies link it with **enhanced alertness, focus and memory**. Some compounds present in rosemary can protect our nervous system and brain from various forms of damage caused by oxidation and over-exhaustion. Not only can it protect the brain from these forms of damage, but it has also been known to heal brain tissue damage caused by a shortage of blood supply to the brain (ischemia). Paired with the herb's ability to prevent the formation of amyloid plaques, rosemary is an essential herb for the elderly, as it can also protect against Alzheimer's disease and dementia.

Rosemary has a direct effect on salivary cortisol. By reducing this stress hormone, it can **improve one's mood while relieving anxiety and stress**. Furthermore, it has been shown that the inhalation of the scent of rosemary helps to clear the mind and relieve tension. When ingested, these effects are enhanced, as rosemary balances our hormones, promoting physical and mental wellbeing.

Rosemary can also **improve digestion and oral health**. By preventing constipation, flatulence and bloating, and by encouraging peristaltic movements of the bowels, it can increase the chances of you absorbing the nutrients you consume. This is essential to our health, as a poor digestive system may lead not only to malnourishment, but to reduced appetite as a result of fear of pain and being uncomfortable. The antibacterial properties also calm the stomach and mouth, which can freshen breath.

By improving blood flow and the production of red blood cells, rosemary can **reduce fatigue** and keep you feeling energised while also improving heart health and reducing the risk of heart disease. As a natural painkiller, it also helps to relieve aches, pains and migraines.

Once thought of as an elixir of youth, rosemary can **reduce the signs of ageing** on the skin as it contains essential oils, which reduce blemishes, improve the health and appearance of the skin and protect against various forms of skin damage. As a natural anti-inflammatory, rosemary can not only prevent the appearance of skin irritations, but actually reduce and remove them altogether.

For those trying to control their weight, rosemary is naturally anti-hyperglycaemic and can **improve the body's metabolic rate**. The greatest results for weight loss caused by rosemary have come from rosemary extracts.

NUTRITIONAL VALUE

Rosemary contains good amounts of vitamins A, B9 and C as well as calcium, iron and manganese. It is also a good source of fibre and contains lower levels of vitamins B1, B2, B6, copper and magnesium.

BASIL

....

(OCIMUM BASILICUM)

PERFECT FOR PIZZAS AND PASTA DISHES,
AS WELL AS THE MAIN INGREDIENT IN
PESTO, BASIL CAN ALSO HELP TO KEEP
US YOUNG. IT'S OFTEN REFERRED
TO AS 'THE ROYAL HERB'.

ORIGIN OF THE SPICE AND HISTORY

There is some question about the origin of basil, but most think the plant is native to India, where it was sacred, and it is thought to have been cultivated for over 5,000 years. It was believed that basil had the power to protect and was therefore planted around temples and graves. Hindus also used to link basil to the gods and use it in their divine blessings.

Throughout history, basil has been used in medicine. One example of this was the use of it in the practice of Ayurveda, an ancient Indian medicinal system. It was commonly prescribed to improve digestion, treat headaches, fight the common cold and increase mental awareness and processing. The herb is still used today in aromatherapy and holistic healing.

Basil was considered an aphrodisiac and a sexual performance enhancer for centuries in Italy. It was once regarded as a a symbol of love, as the scent of basil alone was said to be enough to increase sexual arousal.

In 1820, John Keats wrote a poem called 'The Pot of Basil' (also known as 'Isabella'), in which Isabella's lover was killed by her brothers. Isabella then buried his head in a pot of basil, where she mourned him obsessively.

FOLKLORE

The first part of the Latin name for basil, 'Ocimum', is said to have originated from Greek mythology. It was said that when Ocimus the combat tactician was killed, basil appeared. The second part, 'basilicum', is said to come from the Greek word 'basilikon', meaning royal.

Several cultures have a variety of unrelated beliefs when it comes to basil. The Portuguese, Italians and Romanians have suggested it is linked with romance and fidelity, but other Europeans once linked the herb to the devil.

Basil has been used by many cultures throughout history as a tool for aiding those in the afterlife. Some Europeans used basil in funeral rituals to ensure a safe passage to the afterlife, by placing it in the deceased's hands. India had a similar ritual, but they would place basil in the mouth of the deceased.

HOLISTIC BENEFITS OF BASIL

Basil aids in blood vessel function, which in turn **promotes healthy blood pressure** as it reduces the chance of blood clots forming, which can lead to cardiac arrest and stroke. Basil has high levels of beta-carotene, making it great in the prevention and treatment of heart disease. It is its antioxidant properties that make it effective in blood sugar management, which is important for those suffering with diabetes.

Sleeping regularly is recognised as one of the most important ways to maintain healthy brain and body functionality. The magnesium in basil is thought to improve blood flow and **aid healthy sleep**.

The effects of ageing can be reduced with basil, as it has great antibacterial and antioxidant properties, which can **reduce the visible signs of ageing** by aiding in the maintenance of skin elasticity and reducing wrinkles and age spots. The antibacterial properties also play a role in the reduction and **prevention of acne** and skin soreness and can even help in the healing of acne scars.

The anti-inflammatory effects of basil, **aid digestion and improve bowel conditions**. The reduction of bloating, stomach cramps and acid reflux have all been linked with basil consumption. Its antiseptic properties also make basil effective in the treatment of wounds and ulcers, and there is some evidence that suggests it is effective at reducing stomach worms and parasites. Basil is also used in various cough medicines, which proves its use as an expectorant, and makes it useful in the **treatment of bronchitis and asthma**.

Sexual performance and libido are enhanced by basil, as it decreases the levels of stress and depression hormones in the body and promotes healthy blood flow and metabolism. Basil has also been shown to **regulate hormones**, which make us feel happy and energetic as it directly impacts the neurotransmitters in the brain.

Kidney function can also be strengthened by the consumption of basil leaves. It has been suggested to be most effective when consumed with water on an empty stomach. Kidney stones have also been shown to improve when taking basil as an elixir mixed with honey, over a period of time.

NUTRITIONAL VALUE

Basil is high in vitamins A and K, folate and manganese. It also contains a good amount of vitamins B2, B3, B6 and C, calcium, iron, magnesium, phosphorus, potassium and zinc.

MASTIC

....

(PISTACIA LENTISCUS)

MASTIC IS THE RESINOUS GUM THAT COMES FROM THE
SCORED BARK OF A MASTIC TREE. THE NAME MASTIC
DERIVES FROM THE GREEK WORD 'MASTICHON', WHICH
MEANS TO CHEW. IT IS USED IN BREADS AND CAKES
OR CAN BE CHEWED ON ITS OWN.
IT ALSO KEEPS US YOUNG,
AND IS OFTEN CALLED
'THE GREEK SPICE'.

ORIGIN OF THE SPICE AND HISTORY

Mastic is native to the Greek island of Chios. It is thought that mastic gum has been enjoyed since at least 500 BC, and Dioscorides even mentioned the medicinal and cosmetic benefits of mastic use in the first century AD. It is also thought that the upper-class ladies of the Roman Empire used mastic in their cosmetic creams to cleanse and revitalise the skin.

Mastic is known have become internationally popular during the thirteenth century, after the Genoans conquered Chios. This is when its production increased and its trade grew around Europe. During the thirteenth century, production and distribution were increased, but in order to maintain a high price, excess supplies were often burned or kept for use in later years.

The Ottoman Empire took control of Chios in the sixteenth century and subsequently, the production and distribution of mastic. During the nineteenth century, the value of mastic had fallen from the extortionate price it once held, which led to the formation of the Gum Mastic Growers Association. This organisation allowed growers to come together to share resources, in order to reduce the costs of production and manage the mastic trade.

Today, mastic is not only used as a gum but as a powder and in capsule form for its many health benefits – it has even been used in toothpaste. In the kitchen, mastic is commonly used for baking bread and biscuits as well as confectionery, and in a unique ice cream, which is somewhat chewy.

FOLKLORE

It was believed for a time that the mastic tree's resin was a gift from Saint Isidore, who was martyred in 25 AD – it is thought that the shrub cried tears of gum after watching her torture.

During the Byzantine Empire, mastic was used to scent soaps and was also placed on the skin as a form of sun protection. It was also thought that mastic would provide various health benefits, including increases in sexual desire, restful sleep, a natural antidepressant and the preservation of youthful looks and beauty.

Mastic gum found a role in dentistry, where it was used to fill cavities, cleanse the mouth and create impressions.

Mastic resin has been used throughout history as a treatment for skin conditions and wound healing. In modern times, mastic is used in bandages and adhesive plasters.

CULTIVATION OF MASTIC

Unlike many herbs and spices that are cultivated from the leaves and roots of plants, mastic is carefully extracted from tree bark. The mastic tree is quite particular about where it will grow and prefers soil containing calcium carbonate. It can take up to 50 years before the mastic tree is fully grown and it starts to produce mastic gum in its fifth year of life.

HOLISTIC BENEFITS OF MASTIC

It's no wonder that after millennia as a **digestive aid**, scientific research has confirmed the substantial benefits of mastic for the digestive system. It is still being used in medical concoctions around the world, as it can prevent and reduce the effects of various gastrointestinal disorders while also working as a pain management aid for conditions such as stomach ache and indigestion.

In dentistry, mastic has been known to **strengthen the teeth and gums**, which is essential for preventing tooth decay and maintaining oral health as we age. Not only can this wonderful substance be used for fillings and tooth moulds, but it also eliminates and inhibits the formation of microbial plaque while inhibiting bacteria growth.

There are several ways in which mastic oil can drastically enhance the health of your skin. By boosting collagen, mastic can **prevent wrinkles** and the appearance of photo-aged skin by increasing elasticity. Furthermore, mastic oil is a natural moisturiser that reduces the shiny appearance of oily skin. The antibacterial, anti-inflammatory and antifungal properties of mastic oil also help in the reduction of several skin conditions, including blemishes, blackheads and acne.

The high levels of zinc contained in mastic have been linked with an **increased libido** in men. This is due to increase of prostate functionality, which is caused by chewing mastic gum.

Wound healing is vastly enhanced by mastic resin. This natural healer can be applied directly to the skin to increase your healing rate. Not only will it help rebuild your skin but it may also prevent wound infections.

Mastic **stimulates the liver**, enhancing its detoxifying abilities. This will benefit the entire body, as the liver filters out harmful toxins absorbed from our food and the environment.

LIBIDO

Libido is one of the things most likely to be affected when we are tired or run-down. If we feel good about ourselves, it is easier to fancy some quality 'we' time.

Before we get into the science, it is essential to recognise that in order to naturally increase libido using foods, making time for yourself and feeling comfortable and confident is just as important.

Recent studies have discovered that as we age, our natural libido decreases by around 1 per cent each year. It is logical to think that for people who live an unhealthy lifestyle of drinking, smoking, poor sleeping patterns and an unhealthy diet full of sugar and salt, this number will be much greater. For the rest of us the natural decrease in libido is an understandable decline – but it needn't decline at all. Our libido is controlled by a combination of brain chemistry and bodily reactions. Oxygen and hormone transportation are essential for a healthy libido – the better our blood runs, the better we will feel in the moment, and the better we will perform.

Using herbs and spices, it is possible to make sure our brain and body are performing at their optimum level, which will increase our arousal and help us maintain a healthy libido throughout our lives. Though I do not want to dwell on the negatives, cutting out the alcohol and cigarettes can make an earth-shattering amount of differences as these not only hinder your ability to become aroused, but they block the healthy nutrients you consume, which would otherwise help to increase libido. Try a seven-day detox and see if you (and your partner) can feel a difference.

ESSENTIAL VITAMINS AND MINERALS

VITAMIN A is essential for hormone production in men and women and aids the healthy functioning of the sex organs. Deficiency can lead to testicular and ovarian atrophy. Foods rich in vitamin A include carrots, sweet potatoes, winter squash, cantaloupe melon, apricots, spinach, kale and other leafy greens.

B-COMPLEX VITAMINS are essential for libido and sexual function. These mood-enhancing vitamins keep our brains and nervous systems working at their optimum level, especially when spontaneous bursts of energy are required. B vitamins have also been known to increase blood flow to the genitals and intensify the orgasm in men and women. Deficiencies lead to lower sex drive, less sensitivity of the sexual organs and abnormal hormone levels. Rich sources of B vitamins include poultry, fish and nuts.

VITAMIN C is important in the production of sex hormones which cause arousal, including androgen, oestrogen and progesterone. This vitamin also strengthens the immune system and the blood vessels responsible for carrying blood around the body and to the sex organs, aiding with stronger erections. Excellent sources include citrus fruit, mango, papaya, watermelon, strawberries, green and red cabbage, broccoli and tomatoes.

VITAMIN D aids in the production of sex hormones. This vitamin also strengthens muscles, bones and the immune system, keeping us feeling stronger and enhancing our sexual performance. Foods such as tuna, mackerel, cheese and egg yolks are high in vitamin D.

VITAMIN E is important for increasing testosterone levels. It can also enhance sperm count and mobility, and strengthens the sperm and egg cell. The antioxidant properties in vitamin E also make it essential for removing free radicals from the sex glands while increasing their circulation in the body. It may also reduce menopausal and premenstrual syndrome symptoms, which can get in the way of libido. Good sources include sunflower seeds, almonds, hazelnuts and avocado.

IRON is essential for the maintenance of energy levels and the transportation of oxygen in the blood. Iron deficiency leads to loss of sexual appetite, fatigue and depression. Foods rich in iron include shellfish, spinach, liver and other offal, legumes, quinoa, turkey and broccoli.

MAGNESIUM enhances the production of sex hormones, which increase libido. Many of the herbs and spices used historically as aphrodisiacs have been found to contain some level of magnesium. This mineral is also said to help get you in the mood by relaxing you. It can help in muscle contractions during ejaculation and reduces the risk of muscle cramps. It can be found in dark chocolate, avocado, nuts, legumes, tofu, seeds, salmon, wholegrains, mackerel and bananas.

SELENIUM is important for sperm production and the protection of sperm and eggs. Men lose selenium when they ejaculate and this needs to be replaced. Men carry almost half their selenium in their testicles and seminal ducts. Brazil nuts, pineapple, sweet potatoes, brown rice and chickpeas contain good amounts of this mineral.

ZINC has been found to increase sexual desire by increasing levels of the sex hormones in the body. A deficiency in zinc can lead to an imbalance of oestrogen and progesterone, which may affect sexual desire. It may also hinder the body's response to stress, which may affect sexual stamina. Zinc is thought to be at its highest levels in the prostate gland. Excellent sources include red meat, legumes, seeds, cashews and almonds.

NUTMEG

....

(MYRISTICA FRAGRANS)

THIS SPICE HAS A DISTINCTIVE FRAGRANCE
AND A SLIGHTLY SWEET TASTE, WHEN EITHER
USED AS A WHOLE SEED OR IN GROUND
FORM. IT IS ALSO GREAT FOR
YOUR SEX DRIVE.

ORIGIN OF THE SPICE AND HISTORY

Nutmeg originated from the Molucca islands, which are now part of Indonesia. It is produced by an evergreen tree along with mace, though nutmeg is sweeter and has a stronger aroma.

There is evidence of the use of nutmeg as far back as the first century when it was mentioned by Pliny. It is thought that he regarded nutmeg as a valuable spice for its medicinal qualities. Other ancient texts regarding nutmeg as a beneficial medicine were those of the Vedic literature, which stated that nutmeg was useful for reducing fevers, alleviating headaches and reducing bad breath.

Historically a medicine before it was a baking spice, nutmeg was – and is – still used in a variety of foods. The Italians and the Dutch use nutmeg to flavour their vegetables, stews and desserts. Other popular uses of nutmeg today include the sprinkling of it over hot drinks. It is also used in a variety of desserts, including spice cake and as a warming addition to a pie filling.

FOLKLORE

Historical writing from Arabia identifies nutmeg as an aphrodisiac and a stomach medicine. This is reinforced by ancient Roman and Indian texts, which also regarded nutmeg as a medication. In addition, the Romans used nutmeg as incense.

There have been many suggestions that nutmeg has the ability to clear one's mind and encourage restful sleep. In the practice of Ayurveda, it is a sleeping and digestive aid.

Pregnant women might do well to avoid eating lots of nutmeg – it was once thought of as a self-abortion medication in the Middle Ages, and has been found to be toxic in high amounts. At this time, people also realised that taking nutmeg in high doses could produce hallucinations, due to the amphetamine and mescaline found in the spice.

Like many spices, nutmeg has a place historically in spells. It was once thought that a woman would fall in love with any man who managed to sprinkle nutmeg into her shoe at midnight. Furthermore, the love spell would be enhanced if two people shared a drink containing nutmeg.

HOLISTIC BENEFITS OF NUTMEG

Nutmeg has been known to improve skin condition and reduce the signs of ageing. Not only can it reduce inflammation of the skin, but it also improves skin hydration and elasticity, keeping wrinkles, fine lines and sagginess at bay. Being both antibacterial and antifungal, nutmeg can help in various skin conditions, including acne.

Digestive health can be greatly enhanced by the consumption of nutmeg. Several components of it have been known to inhibit gas and to prevent gastritis, while providing smoother digestion and regulating bowel movements.

Nutmeg is also good for heart health. The iron present in it helps in the production of red blood cells. The potassium in nutmeg can also relax the blood vessels, which will facilitate blood circulation.

Oral health can be improved by nutmeg, as it contains a vast array of antibacterial properties that not only protect the teeth and gums from bacteria, but also provide a defence against cavities and bleeding gums.

Nutmeg can also promote bone density and strength, as it contains several nutrients essential for bone health. The calcium in nutmeg may prevent and be beneficial in the treatment of osteoporosis, too.

Some of the various unique phytochemicals found in nutmeg are thought to stimulate areas of your brain and can decrease depression and increase libido by aiding hormone production. The nutrients in nutmeg can also enhance mental wellbeing and decrease levels of insomnia, relieving nerve tension and increasing serotonin and melatonin production, which can help in restful sleep.

NUTRITIONAL VALUE

Nutmeg contains various essential nutrients, including several B-complex vitamins and vitamins C and A, as well as manganese, copper, magnesium, iron, calcium, phosphorus, zinc and potassium.

CUMIN

·······························

(CUMINUM CYMINUM)

THIS SPICE HAS A NUTTY AND SLIGHTLY
PEPPERY TASTE, AND IS OFTEN MIXED WITH
OTHER SPICES IN CURRY. IT IS KNOWN AS
'THE SEED OF THE GODS' AND CAN ALSO
HELP TO INCREASE LIBIDO.

ORIGIN OF THE SPICE AND HISTORY

The exact origin of cumin not known, but is said to have come from Iran, the Mediterranean or Egypt, with some suggesting that the Nile Valley was the place where it was first found.

One of the earliest uses of cumin is reported to have been in the mummification of the Egyptian Pharaohs. This is one of the reasons cumin was nicknamed 'the seed of the gods' – it dates back almost 5,000 years, making it one of the oldest spices on earth.

During ancient times in India, cumin is said to have been used both medicinally and in the kitchen. This was also true of Roman and Greek cuisines – in fact, the ancient Greeks were reported to have kept little pots of it on the dinner table.

Several reports have suggested that cumin was grown in many Medieval monasteries, where it was used for its nutritional and medicinal values.

Cumin was introduced into South America by the Spanish and Portuguese colonisation of the continent, where it became popular in local cuisine. The spice lost popularity after the Middle Ages, but has regained it during the past century, through an increased interest in Indian, Mexican and Mediterranean cuisine.

FOLKLORE

Several cultures, from the ancient Egyptians to the Romans and Greeks would use this seed to heal the sick and as a natural aphrodisiac. The effect of cumin on arousal is said to intensify when it is taken with honey and black pepper. In India it was once thought that cumin stimulated the base chakra, which in turn would increase desire.

Throughout the Middle Ages, cumin was linked to fidelity and love. For this reason, people were told to keep cumin seeds in their pockets when attending weddings, in order to bless the betrothed couple. Some would even suggest that cumin placed in wine would create a love potion, which would ignite passion in couples who consumed the concoction together.

It was also said that cumin had the ability to stop lovers from wandering – when soldiers went to war, it became a tradition for wives to bake their husbands a loaf of cumin bread, to stop them from straying while they were away.

HOLISTIC BENEFITS OF CUMIN

Cumin has been found to be effective in promoting many elements of healthy digestionas a result of compounds such as cumin aldehyde and thymol, which increase the release of digestive proteins and pancreatic enzymes, which help break up the food and help to release bile and enzymes. It also relieves uncomfortable feelings caused by gas and can be a treatment for nausea and stomach pains, particularly when consumed with hot water. Its digestive properties also help to reduce and prevent diarrhoea, constipation and haemorrhoids. Due to the antiseptic, antibacterial, and antifungal benefits of cumin, it can help to speed up digestion, which aids weight loss.

Cumin can reduce the signs of ageing, internally and externally. It has been found to help in the maintenance of healthy skin by reducing wrinkles and ageing spots, as well as reducing inflammation.

As an excellent source of iron, cumin increases energy levels by preventing and reducing anaemia.

Women during menstruation, breastfeeding and pregnancy can all benefit from cumin consumption. The iron present replaces that lost during menstruation, reducing the risk of anaemia and fatigue. This can help keep a woman's menstrual cycle more regular. It has also been found that women who regularly consume cumin seeds have lower levels of pain during menstruation and milder symptoms of PMS. Children can also benefit from cumin, as iron is essential to their growth and energy levels.

The spice is also great for the immune system and for fighting the common cold. When taken with vitamin C, the iron present in cumin can boost your body's natural immune function. Some evidence has shown that it can even reduce the symptoms of bronchitis and asthma by preventing the build-up of phlegm and mucus.

There are several things in cumin that can reduce stress and anxiety, as well as having a tranquil effect on the mind. This spice can help us to better manage stress as well as helping us to unwind at the end of a long day. This reduces the chance of insomnia and promotes healthy sleep.

Evidence has shown that cumin can help regulate blood sugar levels and blood flow, which makes cumin effective for the prevention and management of diabetes.

Finally, cumin is a very effective libido booster. Not only does the zinc present in the spice help sperm production, there is some evidence that cumin can relieve erectile dysfunction and premature ejaculation, as it gives your blood a boost of vitamins and minerals. If that's not enough, this little seed can help reduce the painful swelling in breasts and testicles, as well as relieving inflammation and pain throughout the body.

Cumin consumption can also help to reduce symptoms of dementia and actively helps memory and everyday cognitive function. This is due to the enhanced blood flow that is caused by an increase in haemoglobin production.

NUTRITIONAL VALUE

Cumin contains high levels of iron, magnesium, manganese and calcium. It also contains phosphorus, zinc, potassium and vitamin B1, as well as vitamins A, E and other B-complex vitamins.

GINGER

························

(ZINGIBER OFFICINALE)

ALSO KNOWN AS 'THE WARMING SPICE',
GINGER IS EXCELLENT WHEN ADDED TO A
STIR-FRY AND CAN BE RELIED ON TO
GENERALLY KEEP THINGS SIZZLING.

ORIGIN OF THE SPICE AND HISTORY

Ginger is a warm, aromatic spice, which is believed to have originated in the rainforests of Southeast Asia, though some dispute this and claim that it actually originated in China. It is said to have been used for more than 5,000 years, making it one of our oldest known spices.

There are several reports of ginger coming to Europe in the eleventh century – the British were said to have relished the spice due to its warming properties in their cold climate. Evidence suggests that by the fifteenth century it had made its way to the Caribbean and South America, where Jamaica, Mexico and Brazil are all reported to have successfully cultivated it.

Throughout history, ginger has been used by different cultures as a cure for various conditions. Fishermen would chew it to relieve and prevent sea sickness, while the Japanese used it as an antidote for fish poisoning, which is one of the reasons ginger became popular when serving sushi. In modern times, over half of all Asian herbal remedies still contain ginger, and it is highly valued as a natural medicine. Ginger is also a key ingredient in Indian and Asian cuisne.

FOLKLORE

The Sanskrit word *'singabera'*, meaning 'horn shaped', is where ginger is thought to have originally got its name.

Some texts suggest that Alexander the Great introduced ginger to the Western world and evidence implies that ginger first came to Greece during the Spice Trade Age.

Ginger was believed by several cultures to be an aphrodisiac, which increases blood flow. The *Kama Sutra* even suggests that ginger directly arouses sexual energies, making it an essential spice for reaching one's sexual potential.

There are some that believe that ginger has magical properties. Some modern witches use it as the main ingredient in love potions, and yet others believe that it can be used in any spells cast to help things move faster, such as the growing of plants. Baked goods containing ginger would not spoil as fast as those without, and although this was likely due to the preservative qualities of the spice, some people assumed that this was further evidence of its magical properties.

HOLISTIC BENEFITS OF GINGER

Ginger consumption has been shown by some studies to **lower cholesterol** by reducing cholesterol absorption in the blood, which may also prevent the formation of internal blood clots. There is also evidence that when ginger is taken alongside onion and garlic the conbination stimulates the pancreas, which decreases cholesterol.

Upset stomachs are widely treated with ginger and ginger tea. Those who suffer from poor digestion and sensitive stomachs often benefit from a cup of ginger tea after each meal. Ginger has also been helpful in reducing symptoms of flatulence, heartburn and bloating. This is due in part to its fantastic antibacterial properties, which have also been shown to fight harmful bacteria, such as Staphylococcus.

Due to its antioxidant properties, ginger can help the body slow down some of the signs of ageing, by reducing the number of free radicals in the body. The potassium that ginger contains also helps to reduce signs of **muscle stiffness and weakness,** as well as aiding kidney function.

Rheumatoid arthritis and **osteoarthritis** can be reduced by ginger consumption, due to its fantastic anti-inflammatory properties. Studies have shown that it can also reduce the pain and symptoms of arthritis and even prevent the disease.

Pain management is essential for those suffering with bone, joint or muscle soreness. For most people in the modern world painkillers seem to be the main choice, though they are not without side effects. Ginger is an exceptional natural form of pain relief, so much so that some studies have likened it to Ibuprofen, but without the side effects.

Cardiovascular health can be improved by ginger – studies identify a regulation and reduction in heart rate, as well as an increase in the strength of the contractions in the upper chamber of the heart for those consuming it. Ginger can also help prevent the build-up of blood clots.

The **immune system** is often strengthened by ginger, and the spice has been used to treat colds, flu and coughs, because it warms up the respiratory tract. It has also been used to treat infections and open wounds, as well as being an anti-parasitic, antiseptic and lymph-cleansing spice.

Blood circulation is improved by ginger and symptoms for related diseases such as Raynaud's disease can be relieved. This is because the spice promotes blood flow to those areas of the body, such as fingers, which are often left cold due to poor blood circulation. The spice has also been found to aid in blood sugar regulation, which can help those who suffer with diabetes.

Libido can also be enhanced by ginger consumption, as its antioxidant properties promote blood flow to the sexual organs.

Motion sickness has for centuries been relieved by the use of ginger. Recent studies have identified how the spice disrupts the feedback between the stomach and nausea centre in the brain by absorbing stomach acid and increasing stomach activity. Some studies also found ground ginger to be more effective than **anti-nausea** medication at reducing motion sickness. Ginger has also been used to alleviate the nausea caused by chemotherapy, morning sickness and hangovers.

NUTRITIONAL VALUE

Though not particularly rich in vitamins and minerals, ginger does contain a fair amount of vitamin B6, magnesium, manganese and potassium.

MOOD FOOD

We all need a pick-me-up from time to time. Unlike hormone balance, which is about making sure your body is running at its optimum level, mood food is about eating certain herbs and spices that give you an emotional lift by releasing endorphins from your brain. One example of this is spicy food that contains chilli. By eating it, you might be left feeling more satisfied after a meal and the heat may also convince your brain that you are doing something dangerous, which would flood your body with endorphins.

When people go grocery shopping, they don't walk down the aisles thinking, 'I could really do with some tryptophan tonight, and perhaps an increase in serotonin tomorrow night, as it's going to be a tough day at work', but this is what our mind is subconsciously doing as we consider the different foods on offer. Though we often respond differently to confectionery and takeaway foods, which are packed with fats and sugar, it's possible to get the same hit from herbs and spices such as cinnamon, ginger, black pepper and even mint, as they have the same effect on the brain, but don't harm us like many of the foods we associate with' feeling good' will. They will also help to reduce our cravings for unhealthy food, as our bodies will be flooded with feel-good chemicals. Eating to improve your mood can be healthy and fun, but it can also keep depression away and help us deal more effectively with stress and anxiety.

ESSENTIAL VITAMINS AND MINERALS

B-COMPLEX VITAMINS are essential for boosting the feel-good factor in all of us. They are vital for maximum functionality of the brain and nervous system. A deficiency in B vitamins has been linked with depression, anxiety and several mental disorders, including schizophrenia. Studies have also shown that these vitamins are natural mood enhancers and often work well as antidepressants by lifting our mood and reducing our stress levels. B vitamins have also been known to regulate our social behaviours and prevent feelings of paranoia. Foods rich in these vitamins include poultry, eggs, legumes and peanuts.

VITAMIN C boosts progesterone levels, which helps reduce feelings of depression and anxiety. As an antioxidant and immune system booster, it keeps us feeling at our best and picks us up when we are not. Excellent sources of vitamin C include citrus fruit, melon, broccoli, Brussels sprouts, cauliflower, pineapple, strawberries, peppers, tomatoes and leafy greens.

VITAMIN D is a mood-regulating hormone, which can remove feelings of depression. It has also been linked with seasonal affective disorder (SAD), which affects people in winter when there is less sunlight, a natural source of vitamin D. Foods rich in this vitamin include tuna, mackerel, salmon, cheese and eggs.

CALCIUM deficiency has been linked with the symptoms of premenstrual syndrome. It has also been linked with depression in women. Excellent sources of calcium include seeds, cheese, yogurt, beans, lentils, sardines, almonds and rhubarb.

IRON is essential for maintaining a good mood, as deficiency can lead to fatigue, low muscle strength and lethargic tendencies. There is also a direct link between iron deficiency and depression. Foods rich in iron include shellfish, spinach, legumes, liver and other offal, quinoa and pumpkin seeds.

MAGNESIUM can reduce feelings of irritability and mental confusion. It has also been suggested that low levels of magnesium are linked with stress. Good sources include dark chocolate, avocado, nuts, legumes, tofu, seeds, bananas and mackerel.

ZINC is essential for the health of the cells in the body. Deficiency in the mineral has been known to lead to depression, a weakened immune system and a loss of appetite. Zinc is found in red meat, shellfish, legumes, seeds, cashews, almonds and dairy.

SAFFRON

··

(CROCUS SATIVUS)

THIS SPICE IS USED MAINLY TO SEASON
AND COLOUR FOOD, BUT IT IS ALSO
GREAT FOR LIFTING MOOD.

ORIGIN OF THE SPICE AND HISTORY

Saffron is believed to have originated in Greece, and spread from Crete to other parts of Europe. Early evidence of this spice was found in wall paintings in a Grecian palace, which included images of saffron harvesters in 2000 BC. There is also evidence for the use of saffron in cooking as far back as 1500 BC, when it was said to have been prevalent in Persian cuisine. It was thought at that time to be a potency-enhancing plant.

One of the earliest uses of saffron in medicine is thought to have been as a treatment for cataracts. Through the ages, it has also been a treatment for various ailments and illnesses, including depression and low libido.

After learning about saffron from the Greeks, the Romans considered it to be a luxury spice. After the fall of the Roman Empire, the popularity of saffron subsided for a while, and it was not until the Middle Ages that it began to regain popularity as a medicine and as a spice. It was also popular as a dye and mood enhancer at that time.

FOLKLORE

The name saffron is said to have derived from the Arabic word 'za'faran', which means 'yellow'.

There are several mythologies surrounding the origination and uses of saffron. Greek mythology sometimes claimed that Zeus slept on a bed of the spice, while Hermes, the messenger of the gods, was said to have unintentionally injured his friend Crocos and, when he saw the stain of blood on the floor that had fallen from the head of his friend, he changed it into the flower bearing saffron.

Saffron has been used in healing throughout the ages. Some of the ailments it has been used to treat include measles, bladder, kidney and liver disorders and even diabetes. Saffron was also prescribed as an aphrodisiac as it was found to reduce sexual dysfunction and low sexual appetite.

HOLISTIC BENEFITS OF SAFFRON

The nutrients contained in saffron make it fantastic at increasing the body's natural defence against illness and injury by **boosting the immune system**. Saffron also helps to create white blood cells, which are essential to fighting off illness. By increasing blood circulation and reducing cholesterol build-up, minerals such as iron increase energy levels while preventing anaemia and also increase metabolic rate, encouraging weight loss. These factors all contribute to a healthy cardiovascular system, which not only prevents conditions such as atherosclerosis but drastically increases the body's recovery rate after illness.

One of the original uses of saffron was as a **digestion aid**. Many spices help digestion, but the sedative qualities found in saffron enhance its ability to calm the stomach and relieve flatulence, constipation and cramps. Saffron may also coat the outer layers of the stomach, which can reduce acid reflux and colic. There is also a belief that it can reduce the suffering of those with **gastric ulcers**.

There is evidence that saffron can improve **bone health,** by increasing the absorption of calcium. Paired with the nutrients present in saffron, this spice can help prevent the onset of osteoporosis and aid in the strength and maintenance of healthy bones.

Saffron has **antidepressant** and **mood-enhancing** qualities. Studies have shown it can cause a reduction in major depressive symptoms when consumed regularly. As the compounds in it stimulate hormone production, saffron enhances the endocrine system and has also been linked with an increase in libido, particularly in women. Saffron can also **improve memory** and could help prevent several brain disorders, including dementia.

NUTRITIONAL VALUE

Saffron is a great source of manganese and also contains iron, magnesium, potassium, copper, calcium, phosphorus, selenium, vitamins C, A and several B-complex vitamins including B2, B3, B6, B9.

CACAO

....

(THEOBROMA CACAO)

THIS POWDER IS AN EASY WAY TO GET THE
COMFORTING, RICH FLAVOUR OF CHOCOLATE
INTO YOUR COOKING AND INSTANTLY LIFT
YOUR MOOD. IT IS SOMETIMES KNOWN AS
'THE FOOD OF THE GODS'.

ORIGIN OF THE SPICE AND HISTORY

The exact origin of cacao is not known, but it is generally accepted that the cacao tree came from the Amazon rainforests in South America.

It is said that the cacao seed was consumed by ancient civilisations including the Olmecs, the Mayans and the Aztecs from around 1800 BC. There is evidence to suggest that it was eaten before 1900 BC, but the general consensus is that the first proven use of cacao was in a drink made by the Olmecs in South America .

Betrothed Mayans were said to have shared a beverage of cacao during their wedding ceremony, which may have been the earliest link of chocolate and romance, a tradition that still flourishes today. Many cultures in the world still associate chocolate with celebrations and love. The taste has come a very long way from the bitter drink created almost 4,000 years ago, to the sweet chocolate we enjoy today.

FOLKLORE

The Mayans believed that cacao was a food of the gods and would depict their gods consuming a chocolate drink. Originally, due to its sacred origins, it was thought that only priests should drink it, but this was eventually extended to include priests and the wealthy. Drinking chocolate was used in several religious ceremonies, from weddings to funerals, for its spiritual power. The Mayans also celebrated a festival in April to honour the god Ek Chuah, who was believed to be the god of cacao.

The Aztecs also believed that there were links between cacao and their gods. They said that the god of harvest, Quetzacoatl, had originally brought the cacao tree to earth and shown the people how to cultivate it and make a drink from its fruit. Not many could afford the drink, but it was believed that wisdom and strength were granted to those who consumed it. The Aztecs also forbade women from enjoying the drink, due its stimulating effects.

The Aztec king, Montezuma, was said to have drank a cup of drinking chocolate before every meeting with a lady friend, due to its stimulating properties. This was on top of the fifty-plus cups of cocoa he consumed daily.

HOLISTIC BENEFITS OF CACAO

Regulation of blood pressure and cholesterol is essential for **cardiovascular health** and reduced risk of heart disease, and the high levels of antioxidants and flavonoid components in cocoa improve the elasticity and pressure of blood vessels. Cocoa has also been known to help in the prevention of blood clotting, which can increase the risk of heart attacks and strokes.

Cocoa is a **natural antidepressant** and has also been known to reduce stress levels. Neurotransmitters such as serotonin and tryptophan are thought to bring about feelings of wellbeing and have been found to increase with cacao consumption. By naturally increasing cognitive processes, cocoa may also offer some relief from tiredness.

NUTRITIONAL VALUE

Cacao contains a good amount of iron, manganese and magnesium as well as some calcium, zinc, potassium and fibre. There are also low levels of B-complex vitamins in it.

BLACK PEPPER

···

(PIPER NIGRUM)

ALSO KNOWN AS 'THE KING OF SPICE',
PEPPER IS GREAT FOR ADDING AN EXTRA
LAYER TO THE TASTE OF YOUR FOOD AND
IMPROVING YOUR OVERALL MOOD.

ORIGIN OF THE SPICE AND HISTORY

Black pepper is native to India, where it has reportedly been used in food for over 4,000 years. Peppercorns were valued for their versatility in a lot of ancient cuisines and for their various medicinal properties, too.

One of the earliest uses of black pepper is said to have been in the mummification ceremonies conducted by the Egyptians. It was said that peppercorns were stuffed into the nostrils of pharaoh Ramses II over 2,400 years ago. The *Mahabharata*, an ancient text, also mentioned the spice as a meat flavouring.

For hundreds of years, black pepper has been used as a medication to reduce inflammation and stiffness in the body. The antioxidant properties of the spice have been harnessed by various alternative therapies such as Siddha and Ayurveda, where pepper is used to increase blood circulation, aid in weight loss and clear the sinus passages.

It is said that peppercorns now account for at least 20 per cent of all spice imports, making it one of the most lucrative spices in the world. This is not surprising as pepper is included in almost every cuisine globally.

FOLKLORE

Packed with more than just antioxidants, pepper has been known to heal everything from constipation to gangrene. Hippocrates regularly mentioned it as a key part of his healing repertoire.

The value of black pepper was so high in Europe and the Middle East that it was once known as 'black gold'. In the Middle Ages, it was said that a man's wealth could be measured by his pepper stockpile. The ancient Greeks used pepper as currency and in sacred offerings, paying everything from taxes to ransoms using the spice. During the sixteenth century, it was claimed that dock workers were not permitted to wear clothing with pockets, for fear of them stealing the valuable peppercorns.

HOLISTIC BENEFITS OF BLACK PEPPER

Skin health can be improved and maintained by the use of black pepper. Due to its high level of antioxidants, its consumption can help in reducing signs of premature ageing, such as wrinkles, fine lines and dark spots. Piperine, which is present in black pepper, facilitates pigmentation of the skin, which has led some researchers to suggest the use of black pepper as an alternative treatment for vitiligo. There is also some evidence that black pepper can prevent skin cancer. Black pepper is also known to improve hair health, as its antibacterial and anti-inflammatory qualities can reduce dandruff and revitalise hair when applied directly to the scalp.

There are many aspects of **cardiovascular health** that benefit from the consumption of black pepper. Vitamin C, along with the several other minerals contained in it, help to maintain healthy blood pressure and lower levels of harmful cholesterol in the blood, while increasing levels of good cholesterol. This is essential for reducing the risk of stroke and heart attack.

Black pepper is also excellent for **weight loss and the digestive system**. The nutrients contained in it aid in the breakdown of fat cells and encourage sweating and urination, which helps the body by getting rid of harmful toxins.

Black pepper has been known to offer **relief from sinusitis**. As a natural expectorant, it may also be useful in the treatment of whooping cough and asthma, as it breaks down mucus and phlegm. Its antibacterial properties also make it beneficial for those suffering with blocked noses, colds and coughs.

Those suffering with **rheumatism and arthritis** may benefit from black pepper consumption. As a naturally warming food, it can stimulate circulation and offer pain relief by removing harmful uric acid from the body. The anti-inflammatory properties of black pepper are also helpful in pain management.

Neurological health is also aided by the use of the spice. Research has found that substances in black pepper lower the chance of memory and cognitive impairment and can also enhance the chemical pathways in the brain, which may benefit those suffering with Alzheimer's disease and dementia. Further effects on the brain have been studied, as black pepper's improvements to cognitive function have been known to reduce the symptoms of depression.

NUTRITIONAL VALUE

Black pepper is an excellent source of vitamin K and manganese. It also contains fibre, the vitamins A, B2, B5, B6 and calcium, magnesium, iron, copper and potassium.

HORMONE STABILITY

This is such an important and emotive subject, and I believe that any little help we can get to stabilise, regulate and manage our hormones is worth the effort.

It's important to establish from the beginning that hormone stability is not something we can solve, but rather something that we need to manage throughout our lives. The good news is that we can get better at it, and herbs and spices can make all the difference.

Our brains create hormones all the time. Everything we do, see, hear, touch, taste or smell leads to our brains sending messages around our bodies. These hormonal changes then dictate how we respond to further stimuli, including to people and our environments. They also allow us to deal with danger and pressure, perform above comfortable levels and drive us to be competitive or subservient. With all this going on, how can we take control of our hormones and reduce our mood swing and feelings of agitation?

Before we move on, it's worth mentioning that there are some slight differences between men and women in hormonal balance. Men often have varying levels of testosterone, which dictate mood and behaviour, particularly around potential mates. Both sexes are known to have hormonal imbalances during several stages of their lives, including puberty. Without trying to underplay hormonal problems in men, there are three distinct hormonal rollercoasters that they will never experience (though they may feel like they do when living with someone who does!).

The first significant hormonal rollercoaster is the menstrual cycle – nature's way of preparing women for pregnancy by throwing around a number of hormones designed to increase the chance of conception. Before the possible conception, a woman may feel more aroused and have a heightened sense of smell and taste. This is different for every woman. Then there is premenstrual syndrome (PMS), when some women may find themselves irritable or emotional with no explanation as to why. When hormones realise there was no conception they move on to the next stage. This can be an exhausting process but it is a cycle, which means it never ends, unless the woman goes through one of the other two rollercoasters. The second one is pregnancy, where the hormones once again fluctuate at different stages of the day, week, month and trimester of the pregnancy. There follows a drastic change in hormones post-birth, which can cause depression. The third difference is menopause, which is when a woman no longer experiences a menstrual cycle, as the body has released its final egg for fertilisation. This stage can last for years and again, every woman's experience will be different. For these reasons, it is important for women to stabilise their hormones. This is not to say that men do not need to stabilise their hormones, it is just respecting the barrage of hormone instability that women experience throughout their lives.

What's food got to do with it? Everything! Recent studies have identified that girls in the Western world are having their periods earlier than ever before, with some girls having their first period at just eight years old. This is thought to have been caused by a number of factors, and some experts suggest that it is strongly associated with food. Our bodies are designed to respond to the foods we eat, but the problem is that most junk and processed foods are filled with unnatural hormone-stimulating substances. These are added for flavour, but they are NOT put in food for any other benefit. I know it is not always possible to eat organic foods, but we must be aware of what we put into our bodies. Overweight girls are far more likely to have an earlier first period, in part because of the oestrogen that is produced by an abundance of fat cells. The xenoestrogens contained in many of our foods, often as a preservative, also contribute not only to early onset puberty in girls, but late puberty in overweight boys.

It is essential that we do all we can to equip our bodies with the correct nutrients to regulate hormone imbalances and facilitate healthy hormone production. This will help us not only in the natural hormonal changes we experience, but it may also prevent us from developing depression and feelings of low self-worth. With the correct nutrients, we can experience feelings of joy and hapiness in a much more fulfilling way.

ESSENTIAL VITAMINS AND MINERALS

B-COMPLEX vitamins play an important role in hormone balance. Vitamin B6 can help to remove symptoms such as mood swings and irritability. It can also be effective in reducing levels of premenstrual syndrome (PMS) in women. B-complex vitamins are found in foods such as poultry, fish and nuts.

VITAMIN C can raise progesterone levels, which helps to reduce depression and anxiety. This may also help regulate emotions and promote healthy sleep, which is essential to hormonal balance. Excellent sources include citrus fruit, mango, papaya, watermelon, strawberries, green and red cabbage, broccoli and tomatoes.

VITAMIN D facilitates the production of several hormones, including thyroid. This helps to regulate metabolism and body temperature. Low levels of vitamin D are also linked with hormonal imbalance and depression. Vitamin D may also boost testosterone in men, which is especially important for older men as their levels naturally drop. Foods such as tuna, mackerel, cheese and egg yolks are high in vitamin D.

VITAMIN E has been found to be useful in regulating hormones, particularly in menopausal women and women who have low oestrogen levels. Good sources include sunflower seeds, almonds, hazelnuts and avocado.

MAGNESIUM is known to reduce symptoms of PMS and mood swings. It also plays a role in balancing progesterone. It can be found in dark chocolate, avocado, nuts, legumes, tofu, seeds, salmon, wholegrains, mackerel and bananas.

SELENIUM is crucial to the thyroid gland, which controls metabolism. A deficiency can lead to metabolic rate imbalances. Environmental factors, such as mercury in fish, can disrupt the hormones in the body – selenium can reduce the negative effects of these heavy metals by neutralising them. Brazil nuts, tuna, chicken breasts, shellfish, shiitake mushrooms and wholewheat pasta are excellent sources of selenium.

ZINC is important for the regulation of hormones and can be found in every cell in the body. Zinc deficiencies can lead to several health defects, including hormonal imbalances. Red meat, shellfish, seeds, cashews, pine nuts, almonds, dairy and dark chocolate are rich sources of zinc.

SAGE

(SALVIA OFFICINALIS)

THIS HERB ADDS AN EARTHY FLAVOUR TO
MANY DISHES AND IS KNOWN FOR ITS
STRONG AROMA. ALSO REFERRED TO AS
'THE SAVIOUR HERB', IT IS BELIEVED TO
HELP WITH DEPRESSION.

ORIGIN OF THE SPICE AND HISTORY

Native to the Mediterranean, sage has been used for healing and culinary purposes for millennia. Some of the earliest uses of sage include those of the ancient Egyptians, who are thought to have used it as a painkiller and to treat skin conditions.

Sage tea has links with many cultures, including Greek, Chinese and even Ayurveda. Many cultures boil the leaves for its healing properties.

The Romans recognised the healing properties of sage and included it in their official pharmacopeia. It was used for its ability to aid in digestion, and it was also extensively used by many cultures as a preserver of meat because it is a natural antiseptic.

Today, sage is often combined with onions in a stuffing that accompanies turkey and chicken during festive times.

FOLKLORE

In ancient times it was thought that the smell of sage could ward off evil. Several cultures believed that the daily consumption of sage leaves would keep evil away and attract good into one's life.

The Romans thought so highly of the herb that they associated it with immortality and higher mental processing. Sage has been used throughout history for cleansing, purification and blessings by burning it during various ceremonies.

It was once thought that sage was an essential component in spells to reverse the effects of the 'Evil Eye'. Others would carry it in a purple bag to provide guidance to those making important life decisions.

HOLISTIC BENEFITS OF SAGE

Sage has been used for millennia to relieve and treat the symptoms of colds, flu, coughs, fevers and sore throat. This suggests that it is exceptional at helping the body's natural immune system and aiding in the prevention of many ailments, including hypertension, cardiovascular disease and even those relating to dental health.

Sage can help in reducing the effects of natural ageing by improving the texture of the skin and hair when used externally.

Sage was historically used as an anaesthetic and can aid in pain management. It can also be used as an alternative medicine to treat conditions such a gum disease, cold sores and skin conditions, when applied directly to the affected area. It has also been known to reduce the effects of asthma, when inhaled from a bowl of hot water.

Sage has been proven to reduce and, in some cases, eliminate symptoms of hot flushes in menopausal women due to its hormone-balancing properties. Throughout history it has also been used to treat the symptoms of menstruation and to treat mothers who have excessive milk flow during nursing.

Throughout history, sage has been used to treat digestive problems. This is not surprising, as evidence has identified its ability to treat flatulence, gastritis, diarrhoea, bloating, heartburn and even to improve one's appetite.

If you're having difficulty sleeping, sage tea may help. As a natural sedative, it can promote healthy, natural sleep and can even reduce the feeling of stress. The calming effect produced by sage has also been linked with treating depression. It is important to avoid sage if you are taking sedative medication – the two combined may cause a higher level of sleepiness than is recommended.

NUTRITIONAL VALUE

Sage is an excellent source of vitamin B9, calcium, magnesium, iron, manganese, vitamins A, C, E and K, as well vitamins B1, B2, B6 and B9. It also contains fibre.

TURMERIC

....

(CURCUMA LONGA)

THIS SPICE HAS POWERFUL ANTI-INFLAMMATORY
EFFECTS AND IS A VERY STRONG ANTIOXIDANT.
IT MAKES YOU FEEL GREAT, BOTH PHYSICALLY
AND MENTALLY. IT IS ALSO KNOWN
AS 'INDIAN SAFFRON'.

I have used turmeric for many years and believe it to be a wonder spice. This was proved to me unequivocally this summer. I left the UK for a month and didn't take any turmeric with me, as I didn't have access to a kitchen. Due to that, I couldn't do what I usually do – when in doubt I add a heaped teaspoon of turmeric and a teaspoon of black pepper to pretty much everything I cook – and I was not drinking my usual turmeric lattes. The first week passed without much incident but the after the second week, I noticed my hip was hurting in the morning and I was feeling really stiff. Lots of ailments started to creep up on me – my ankles felt shortened and tight; I was restless at night and I had terrible sleep. My back started aching and my skin got patchy and pigmented. I could not work out why, and then I remembered my lack of turmeric. I started adding it to my daytime routine again and within a week all my ailments were receding. It really is an elixir for good health.

ORIGIN OF THE SPICE AND HISTORY

Turmeric originated in India. It has been used for over 6,000 years and was said to have reached China by 700 AD, East Africa by 800 AD and West Africa by 1300 AD. Arab traders spread the plant to Europe in the thirteenth century.

Turmeric was initially used as a dye and a medicine before becoming a culinary spice. It gives curry its golden colour, and is considered to be holy in India.

Hindu monks historically dyed their robes yellow with turmeric. It was believed to enhance the chakras and body energy, as the colour was associated with the sun; and so turmeric was very important in Hindu and Buddhist spiritualism.

FOLKLORE

There are areas of rural India where it is believed that withholding turmeric from the diet can lead to death by infections.

The Tamil festival Pongal offered a whole turmeric plant to the sun god.

In south India, the spice is used in the puberty ritual during a turmeric bathing ceremony. In some other parts of India, it is believed that if a married woman places turmeric water on her cheeks, evil spirits will not be able to inflict their wicked ways upon her. It is also believed that evil spirits and supernatural beings cannot stand the smell of burning turmeric, so it was burned in Bengal to help identify if a person was a human or a ghost.

HOLISTIC BENEFITS OF TURMERIC

The curcumin in turmeric is anti-inflammatory, antibacterial, antiseptic and antioxidant, making it one of the most health-benefiting spices on the planet.

Turmeric can help reduce the risk of and aid in the treatment of **Alzheimer's disease**. Curcumin, the active ingredient in the spice, blocks some of the beta-amyloid plaque formations that cause Alzheimer's disease. Turmeric is also a natural anti-inflammatory and reduces this in the brain. It has been suggested that turmeric can also help sufferers of multiple sclerosis and Parkinson's disease.

The **digestive system** improves its function with turmeric intake. Some studies have identified a link between turmeric and bile production, which is responsible for promoting digestive health in several ways that include reducing bloating and gas as well as reducing reflux and colon spasms. There are also suggestions that turmeric may also be useful in the treatment of IBS.

Due to its anti-inflammatory properties, turmeric has been recommended for the treatment and prevention of **rheumatoid arthritis**. The anti-inflammatory properties can also aid in healing open wounds and reducing the chance of infection because turmeric inhibits some of the enzymes that encourage pain and swelling in cuts and infections.

There are some links between turmeric intake and the **reduction of blood sugar levels**, which suggests it could be useful in the fight against diabetes.

Turmeric has been known to aid in fighting **depression and relieving stress,** without the addictive side effects of medication.

Turmeric consumption may also reduce the risk of **heart disease and stroke** by decreasing the chance of blood clot formation.

Blood flow is stimulated and increased by turmeric, which has led to it being used to treat menstrual cramps, endometriosis, dysmenorrhea and amenorrhea uterine cysts in women. Turmeric also stimulates uterine contractions and has been used to help reduce anaemia, due to its healing compounds and high iron content.

Regularly drinking turmeric tea can detoxify your body and improve **skin health**. Turmeric also has the ability to remove unwanted toxins from our system – as it flushes out those that lead to weight gain.

Turmeric is an active ingredient in many cough syrups and throat medicines, due to its antibacterial properties that make it effective in fighting certain infections, while its antibacterial and anti-inflammatory properties make it an effective painkiller.

NUTRITIONAL VALUE

Turmeric is high in nutrients and contains high amounts of iron, manganese and vitamin B6. It is also a good source of vitamins B3, C and E, as well as potassium, magnesium, calcium and zinc.

CHILLI

(CAPSICUM)

KNOWN AS 'THE FIERY SPICE', THIS
ADDS HEAT AND FLAVOUR TO JUST
ABOUT EVERYTHING, BUT IT CAN
ALSO IMPROVE YOUR MOOD.

ORIGIN OF THE SPICE AND HISTORY

The chilli plant is native to South and Central America. There are reports that claim the use of chilli as far back as 7500 BC. Archaeological evidence has identified that chilli peppers became a domesticated crop over 6,000 years ago. Some evidence suggests that it was part of Mexican cuisine as far back as 4000 BC, which makes it one of the oldest cultivated crops in the Americas. This fiery fruit is believed to have been originally used as a decorative item, before it was used as a food or medicine. Throughout history, there have been reports of chilli being used as jewellery and even in ancient monuments.

Chilli remained a South American crop for thousands of years, until it was introduced elsewhere during the age of exploration. The Mayan and Aztec civilisations used chilli to cure illness, and there are also reports that these early civilisations used it to fumigate houses. In Aztec culture, chilli would be rubbed on the feet of babies, in order to bring them health and prosperity in life. They would also burn chilli at funerals to keep dark spirits away from the deceased.

Today, chilli is used throughout the world and is said to be eaten by one-quarter of the global population every day. It has also gained popularity as people try to breed hotter and hotter varieties of the fruit, so they can claim the award of the 'hottest chilli in the world'.

FOLKLORE

Before Christopher Columbus arrved in America, shamans there would mix chilli with other plants, in order to aid in spiritual journeys to the other worlds.

Chilli is not for everyone! Scientists have likened eating it to riding rollercoasters or skydiving. The capsaicin in it triggers pain receptors, warning our brain of danger, even though we know we are relatively safe. This releases a wave of endorphins, as our brain tells us that we are doing something dangerous. As is the case with many things, eventually a chilli lover may need more and more heat in order to get the rush of endorphins – we can eventually adapt and tolerate higher levels of heat through regular consumption.

HOLISTIC BENEFITS OF CHILLI

The burning sensation caused by the capsaicin in chilli naturally dilates the blood vessels, which improves **blood circulation** and reduces the risk of several conditions including stroke, blood clotting and heart failure. By increasing the effectiveness of the circulatory system, chilli can also help decrease the amount of cholesterol in the blood.

The boost in circulation combined with a natural **reduction of the insulin in the blood** makes chilli a great form of diabetes management. For those who do not suffer with diabetes, chilli is a great way to prevent the disease, as it naturally lowers blood sugar.

Chilli can promote **healthy weight loss** in a number of ways. Not only does it break down sugars in the blood, but regular consumption can increase the body's metabolic rate by increasing the natural thermogenic progression in our body, which means that more fat is burned. This in turn will aid in the breakdown of foods and fats, which leads to the better absorption of nutrients that help the digestive system as a whole. There is also evidence that consuming chilli for breakfast will keep you feeling fuller for longer.

One way to maintain youthful skin is to eat chilli, as the antioxidants and nutrients are good for maintaining the **skin's elasticity and shine**. The antibacterial properties of it also make it effective in the battle against acne.

Many people experience a lift in their mood after eating chilli, because the capsaicin responsible for giving the chilli heat also sends a rush of feel-good endorphins around your body. For this reason, chilli can be seen as a **natural antidepressant**.

When suffering from a **cold or a blocked nose**, people have often turned to spicy foods for relief. The combination of beta-carotene, capsaicin, high level of vitamin C and some vitamin E make it suitable for this, as the immune system is given a boost while the capsaicin naturally decreases inflammation and congestion of the nasal passages.

NUTRITIONAL VALUE

Chilli is an excellent source of vitamin C. There is also a fair amount of vitamin B6 as well as lower levels of vitamins A, B3, E and K and iron, magnesium and potassium.

SPICE
FOR HEALTH

Staying healthy is key to a long life, and what we put on our plates is a huge part of that. While I am an advocate of conventional medicine and seeing a doctor when we need to, I also believe that we can intervene on our own behalf through what we eat. Various spices can be used to treat illness and ward off specific ailments. They help our body be its best self and can help us manage all sorts of issues, many of which I will examine here.

FERTILITY

A couple of years ago I had a real shock. I'd missed a period and thought it must be the beginning of my menopause. I made an appointment with a gynaecologist to see what was going on and much to my surprise, she told me that not only was I not going through the menopause, but I still had a lot of eggs in my ovaries and was very fertile. She said I still had the fertility of someone in their early thirties. At 47, that really was a surprise.

I wanted to work out why I had such prolonged fertility. Was it genetic or due to my lifestyle? After talking with my family we worked out it was probably not genetic, which left lifestyle. I have exercised regularly and kept my weight in check since my twenties, but I believe it is more a result of my diet, which is mainly a Mediterranean one with lots of fish, fresh fruit and vegetables. Added to that, I believe it is the addition of spices and herbs that have kept me healthy and fertile.

To some evolutionists, reproduction is the answer to 'what is the meaning of life?'. Charles Darwin suggested in his book *The Origin of Species* that we are all driven to survive, and that only the strong will prevail. He wasn't talking about survival in the literal sense but of the survival of genes through reproduction. By this rationale, the meaning of life is not the survival of the fittest, but the survival of the fertile! Simply knowing this should help us realise that nature wants us to reproduce, and has provided us with all the natural substances needed to maximise our reproductive potential. If this were not true, none of us would be here.

In order to understand what makes us more fertile, it's worth considering what makes us less fertile. Smoking, drinking, drug use, obesity, poor diet and low levels of physical activity are among the top culprits. For thousands of years we reproduced without fizzy drinks, processed foods and huge amounts of additives. With herbs and spices provided by nature, we have a strong arsenal of fertility-boosting vitamins and minerals, so it is up to us to provide our bodies with these nutritious ingredients and avoid all the harmful substances.

If you're trying to get pregnant or to produce healthy sperm, before you consume your next harmful substance, think to yourself 'Do I want this to become part of my unborn child's cellular make-up?' And if that doesn't do it, ask yourself 'What would my unborn child choose?' If you think the answer is processed meat, sweets, cigarettes and other types of junk, you are wrong. If you think that one is OK and won't do any harm, you should know that even one is one too many.

In order to increase our chances of conception and have a healthy pregnancy, we need to become the purest vessels we can for our unborn children. After all, we will be hosting our child for nine months, providing them with every nutrient tfor their development. Exercise and get your blood flowing and let evolution know that you're not done yet. When you exercise that is exactly what you are doing, and by doing so you will provide your child with a healthy environment during pregnancy. Keeping active will also help you in the 'art' of conception too, so get moving! Make sure you give your child the best possible nutrition by providing your body with what is necessary to achieve that goal.

ESSENTIAL VITAMINS AND MINERALS

B-COMPLEX vitamins are essential to fertility. Vitamin B6 can increase a woman's luteal phase, which will increase her fertility. This vitamin also increases progesterone levels, which are essential for regular menstruation. Poultry, fish and nuts are rich sources of B vitamins.

VITAMIN B9, also known as folic acid, is extremely important for the development of the child and should be taken before you conceive and throughout the pregnancy. This vitamin also reduces the risk of miscarriage and stillbirth when taken before and during pregnancy. It is also important that men are not deficient in vitamin B9 when trying for a child. This vitamin is found in pork, poultry, fish, peanuts, milk, bread and soya beans.

VITAMIN C is essential to sperm health, as it increases the overall number and strength of the sperm. High levels of vitamin C are also linked with greater mobility among sperm. This vitamin also aids in the regulation of healthy ovarian function and the menstrual cycle and is important for iron absorption. Excellent sources include citrus fruit, mango, papaya, watermelon, strawberries, green and red cabbage, broccoli and tomatoes.

VITAMIN D can help the body with the production of sex hormones. There are also links between vitamin D deficiency and female infertility, as well as polycystic ovary syndrome. Foods such as tuna, mackerel, cheese and egg yolks are high in vitamin D.

VITAMIN E can increase fertility in women and men and is also a powerful antioxidant. It can also improve the cervical mucus and the sperm mobility, maximising the chance of a successful journey of a sperm to the egg. Good sources include sunflower seeds, almonds, hazelnuts and avocado.

IRON can increase fertility by strengthening red blood cells and balancing ovulation. It is extremely important for women trying to conceive and for pregnant women, as iron deficiency is more likely to occur in women, due to menstruation and lactation. The richest sources of iron are shellfish, spinach, liver and other offal, legumes, red meat, pumpkin seeds, quinoa, turkey and broccoli.

SELENIUM is known to improve sperm mobility and formation. In women, selenium assists in the development of ovarian follicles, which leads to the production of healthy eggs. Rich sources include Brazil nuts, shellfish, pork chops, chicken breasts, shiitake mushrooms, prawns and wholewheat pasta.

ZINC is extremely important for the production and balance of sex hormones in women and for boosting the immune system. Being healthy is beneficial to fertility as it means the body is working at its best, preparing for what nature designed it to do – conceive. Sperm development is dependent on zinc and there is a positive correlation between zinc and both sperm count and the strength and maturity of sperm. There are also links between zinc deficiency and early miscarriage. Rich sources of zinc include red meat, shellfish, seeds, cashews, pine nuts, almonds, dairy and dark chocolate.

CLOVES

(SYZYGIUM AROMATICUM)

THEY MIGHT BE SMALL, BUT CLOVES ARE
MIGHTY WHEN IT COMES TO NUTRITIONAL
AND NATURAL HEALTH.

ORIGIN OF THE SPICE AND HISTORY

Clove is native to the Molluca Islands, which were once known as the Spice Islands and are now part of Indonesia. The clove itself is the unripened flower bud of the evergreen clove tree. Once they have been harvested and dried out, this spice is used both whole and ground.

Early evidence of clove use includes an archaeological discovery in Syria from 1721 BC, where they were discovered inside ceramic vessels. Cloves were popular in Europe during the Middle Ages, when one of their main uses was to treat toothache.

Clove cultivation was first introduced to India by the East India Company around the turn of the nineteenth century, where it is was cultivated along with nutmeg in the company's spice garden in Tamil Nadu. Due to the success of clove cultivation there by 1850, clove farming eventually spread to several other regions in India.

Today, cloves are used a culinary spice and a flavouring – some cultures add cloves to tea for an aromatic taste. The eugenol found in cloves is also used in mouthwash. The antiseptic and anaesthetic properties are also harnessed medicinally, particularly in dentistry, and as a natural alternative to medicine.

FOLKLORE

The word clove is said to have originated from the French world 'clou', which means nail, because many people thought cloves looked like nails.

For a time, the Mollucan people would try to plant a clove tree for every child that was born, as they believed that the child and tree would share a fate.

Clove oil is thought to be beneficial for oral and skin health. Clove oil is also common in first aid kits, due to its various antiseptic properties.

Mixing clove with wine or cider is said to maximise its aphrodisiac properties. In friendship, it was thought that if both parties wore a pouch with seven cloves inside it, their friendship would be unbreakable.

HOLISTIC BENEFITS OF CLOVES

Cloves contain eugenol, which is one of the main reasons for its wealth of health benefits. One of the most common uses of cloves is in the treatment of ailments relating to **oral health**. Known to be a **natural anaesthetic**, chewing cloves can significantly reduce toothache, as the oil within the clove numbs the affected area. Cloves can also help get rid of bacteria in the mouth, freshening breath as well as helping to relieve a sore throat due to its antibacterial and anti-inflammatory properties.

The anti-inflammatory properties of cloves also makes them effective in the treatment of **arthritis and joint pain.** Paired with the pain relief they can offer, this wonderful spice should be in the kitchen of anyone who exercises or needs to prevent or recover from joint pain. The eugenol and flavonoids in cloves also aid in the preservation of bone density and reduce the risk of osteoporosis.

Inhaling the scent of crushed cloves can offer relief from **headaches**. The scent is also said to be calming for the mind and can help reduce stress.

Cloves help with **blood sugar regulation**, which is important for the prevention and management of diabetes.

Cloves are also effective in the promotion of a healthy digestive system, as the spice increases the secretion of digestive enzymes, which **reduce flatulence.** The components of clove are thought to protect the stomach lining and can also reduce the effect and risk of stomach ulcers. The fibre in clove is essential for aiding the digestive muscles, which can alleviate constipation.

The antifungal properties of cloves can help to **kill infections** in the body and in the battle against acne. Cloves are effective in the maintenance of healthy skin and the reduction of visible signs of ageing.

There is evidence that cloves can reduce the symptoms of colds and coughs. In oil form, it has been known to be effective in the treatment of bronchitis and asthma.

Cloves have also been found to be effective in the increasing of **libido**. Results showed that the spice was as effective as some modern prescribed medication.

The vitamins and minerals found in cloves make the spice effective for **increasing fertility** in men and women. In men cloves can also increase their testosterone levels and testicular function.

NUTRITIONAL VALUE

Cloves contain a large amount of manganese and high levels of vitamin K. As well as being a source of fibre, cloves also contain potassium, magnesium, iron, calcium, selenium, zinc and vitamin E, and low levels of vitamins C, A, D and some B-complex vitamins.

FENNEL

(FOENICULUM VULGARE)

FENNEL CONTAINS SIGNIFICANT AMOUNTS
OF FIBRE, WHICH DECREASES THE RISK
OF HEART DISEASE AND REDUCES
CHOLESTEROL IN THE BLOOD.

ORIGIN OF THE SPICE AND HISTORY

Fennel is native to the Mediterranean and has been used throughout history. It was popular among the Romans for its texture and taste, but also for its various medicinal properties. Pliny, the Roman writer, used fennel in over 20 medicinal remedies, especially stressing the use of it for the preservation of healthy vision.

In the ninth century, fennel was regarded so highly by the Holy Roman Emperor that it was one of the herbs he demanded was grown in his Imperial Gardens. This was for its suggested healing properties, and not for its culinary uses.

The Anglo-Saxons held fennel in high regard as one of their nine sacred herbs mentioning it in several texts for its culinary and medicinal uses. In thirteenth-century England, it was used to help people get through times of fasting, due to the belief that it was a fantastic hunger suppressant.

Today, fennel is popular in Europe, although it is also used in cuisines all over the world for its fascinating flavour. Germans often prescribe fennel tea for dyspepsia and also use it in cough syrups and stomach remedies.

FOLKLORE

Roman warriors would consume fennel as they believed it would enhance their strength and capability in battle, while also keeping them thin. This is further supported by the Greek word for fennel, 'marathon', which means 'grow thin'. After their success at the Battle of Marathon (known as 'place of fennel'), the Greeks used woven fennel to represent their victory.

Several documents throughout history suggest that fennel is good for the eyes and can prevent blindness. There is also some evidence that properties of fennel can help to prevent macular degeneration.

The Ayurvedic Pharmacopeia of India recommends using dried fennel or the extract of fennel as a medicine to treat various ailments, including anorexia and flatulent colic in children. The ancient Chinese pharmacopeia concurs with this belief.

Western cultures once believed that hanging fennel above doors or placing it inside keyholes would keep away evil spirits and ghosts. This was said to be most effective during the Midsummer's Eve celebration.

HOLISTIC BENEFITS OF FENNEL

The nutrients in fennel help it to reduce harmful levels of cholesterol in the blood, which makes it effective in the **prevention of heart disease**, atherosclerosis and stroke. The potassium in fennel also works as a natural vasodilator, which improves blood flow and reduces blood pressure. Though fennel does not directly affect blood sugar as much as some other spices, it is still an effective treatment for diabetes, due to its ability to reduce blood pressure.

Fennel is a great natural remedy for **anaemia**. Not only does it contain iron, which is essential for the transportation of oxygen in the blood, but the histidine in it stimulates the production of several components in the blood, including haemoglobin. This also makes fennel great for the prevention of fatigue.

As a natural stimulant, fennel aids the digestive system and should be consumed by those who suffer with digestive and stomach problems. It reduces inflammation in the stomach and intestines while also promoting the **absorption and digestion of nutrients.** By stimulating the secretion of digestive fluids and bile production, fennel can also treat constipation, flatulence and various other intestinal problems including IBS.

The calcium and magnesium in fennel makes it effective in promoting **bone health**. It also helps to improve bone strength, which is particularly important for the ageing population.

The vitamin C found in fennel is great for the body's natural **immune system**. Not only does this antioxidant prevent illness, it also aids in the repairing of any damage to the skin and blood vessels, while protecting the cells in the body from oxidative damage.

Fennel has been known to **reduce the symptoms of premenstrual syndrome**. By regulating hormones in the body, it is also effective at treating the pains and anxiety suffered by menopausal women.

Essential for those trying to have a child, fennel is a great source of vitamin B9, which not only promotes the **healthy growth of a child in the womb**, but also drastically reduces the risk of birth defects.

Various studies have linked fennel consumption with the maintenance of **eye health**. Several components found in it contribute to the prevention of premature ageing in the eyes caused by oxidative damage and disorders, such as macular degeneration.

NUTRITIONAL VALUE

Fennel contains vitamins C and A and some B-complex vitamins, as well as calcium, magnesium, iron, magnesium, potassium, manganese, selenium, copper and fibre.

ANISEED

....

(PIMPINELLA ANISUM)

KNOWN AS 'THE DIGESTIVE AID', ANISEED
HELPS TO TREAT BLOATING AND ALSO
IMPROVES THE WAY OUR BODY COPES
WITH THE FOOD WE EAT.

ORIGIN OF THE SPICE AND HISTORY

Aniseed is native to the part of the Mediterranean closest to Southwest Asia and North Africa. It is debatable as to whether Egypt and Greece was the first to discover this spice.

The Greeks and Romans documented the cultivation of aniseed and its medicinal properties as medicine. Around the year 800 AD, the Holy Roman Emperor demanded that it be grown in the Imperial Gardens, to be used as a food and a medicine.

Some of the earliest uses of aniseed were as a digestive aid – it was used to alleviate stomach and intestinal cramps, flatulence and nausea. The effects of aniseed as a mild sedative were also recorded, as it was used to treat anxiety.

Some cultures still use aniseed as a digestive aid, but others have embraced its flavour in food, and it is now used in everything from cakes, cheeses and sweets to breads and pickles.

FOLKLORE

Aniseed is often confused with star anise (*Illicium verum*). However, though they have a similar name and flavour, the two are not the same species of plant.

It is said that the traditional wedding cake we know and love today originated from the spiced cakes baked by the Romans; these were infused with anise and were served at the close of a marriage feast, in order to reduce flatulence and help digestion.

HOLISTIC BENEFITS OF ANISEED

Stomach pain and spasmodic flatulence are both relieved by the use of aniseed, particularly when taken as tea. The seed is a fantastic aid to the digestive system. It has also been known to reduce the symptoms of vomiting, nausea, diarrhoea, abdominal pains and gastritis. The seed is also thought to be effective in preventing microbial infections and some viruses. Its antimicrobial properties also make it great for oral health.

There is evidence that aniseed can help the sufferers of sleep disorders such as insomnia. The essential oils can also calm the mind when taken after meals or before bed. Most commonly consumed as a tea, it is important to not boil the seed for too long, or the essential oils may be significantly reduced in strength.

Many aspects of cardiovascular health can be protected with the use of aniseed. As a substance that removes toxins from the blood and regulates blood pressure, aniseed can help regulate heart beat, which reduces the risk of heart disease.

As an expectorant, aniseed can reduce coughs and even some symptoms of asthma. Anise oil can also aid in the reduction of phlegm in the lungs.

There is also evidence that aniseed encourages healthy menstruation and can reduce menstrual cramps and other symptoms of PMS. The essential oil of anise can also aid in the production of breast milk and has been known to help mothers during labour due to its oestrogenic effects. Aniseed has been known to improve health in babies by reducing stomach pains and hiccups.

B-complex vitamins make aniseed a healthy weight-loss and sleep aid. These vitamins are essential for the breakdown of fats into energy. They have also been known to increase fertility rates and stabilise hormone imbalance.

NUTRITIONAL VALUE

Aniseed is a good source of iron and manganese. There are also fair amounts of vitamin C and B-complex vitamins including vitamins B1, B2, B3, B5 and B6. It also contains calcium, magnesium and potassium, as well as fibre.

INSOMNIA AND FATIGUE

I bet you've never read a book that was trying to put you to sleep! OK, admittedly it's just this section and no, we're not talking about right now, but you get the idea.

We live in a very busy world, full of flashing lights and screens designed to keep us awake. To make matters worse, we're almost always saying we're too busy or we don't have enough time, and by the time you've checked who's liked what and who did what on your social media, you're probably wondering how anybody else ever gets anything done. It's important to recognise these behaviours, as they all lead to insomnia, fatigue and burnout.

We may not be able to shut ourselves out from the busy world we live in, and more than likely, wouldn't want to, but we need to recognise what we can do in order to master our time and not feel like we're missing out. For many people, the present isn't even the problem, as they spend sleepless nights worrying about the future, or overwhelmed by anxieties from the past. If that sounds all too familiar, or if chromic pain or a medical condition keeps you awake at night, the good news is that there are several tried and tested herbal remedies that are known to help. By calming the nerves and relaxing the brain, herbs and spices (and particularly herbal teas) can make a huge difference, as they desensitise us to the abundance of stimuli and reduce our anxieties. These remedies are particularly useful for those who work irregular hours, such as shift workers, or those who work at home during the evenings. These situations disturb the body's natural circadian rhythm, which can increase the chance of insomnia. The brain will typically start producing melatonin at around 9pm, causing relaxation and sleepiness. This release lasts for around 12 hours, but if the body is failing to produce enough melatonin, it can be difficult to get sleepy.

It is true that some people have a disposition to insomnia due to their brain chemistry and have been told to avoid caffeine for eight hours (as that's how long it stays in your system) before bed, have no television or screens in the bedroom and have an hour-long wind down before bed. Though these are all excellent remedies for insomnia, having the extra help from herbs and spices that are proven to relax you can make all the difference. Exercise is also a fantastic remedy for sleep disorders.

It is understandable to see how some people think that fatigue and exhaustion can lead to restful sleep. However, this is far from the truth and can often lead us into a downward spiral of fatigue and insomnia, as one unrestful night leads to an unproductive day, which can cause fatigue, stress and anxiety and lead to another unrestful night. This can be avoided by consuming nutrients designed to help us maintain high energy levels, such as iron and those that help in natural relaxation, such as magnesium. This way we can have productive days of activity, which leave our brain with a sense of achievement. When paired with some exercise and nutrients designed to make you feel relaxed and less anxious, it is likely you will have a better quality of sleep.

ESSENTIAL VITAMINS AND MINERALS

B-COMPLEX VITAMINS have been shown to aid in restful sleep, as they regulate tryptophan production, which is beneficial for the production of melatonin, a natural sleep inducer. These vitamins are also essential for the breakdown of food into energy and can help reduce or eliminate fatigue. Rich sources of B vitamins include poultry, fish and nuts.

VITAMIN C has been known to raise the level of progesterone in the body, which promotes healthy sleep. Excellent sources include citrus fruit, mango, papaya, watermelon, strawberries, green and red cabbage, broccoli and tomatoes.

VITAMIN D can help us get a full night's sleep. Deficiency in this vitamin has been associated with disturbed sleep. It has also been known to reduce aches and pains in the body, as well as lowering levels of fatigue which all help in restful sleep. Tuna, mackerel, cheese and egg yolks are high in vitamin D.

VITAMIN E has been found to help menopausal women sleep, by reducing hot flushes and night sweats. There is also evidence that it reduces restless legs syndrome, which makes people feel a constant need to move their legs at night. Good sources include sunflower seeds, almonds, hazelnuts and avocado.

CALCIUM can also help the brain use tryptophan to create melatonin, a natural sleep inducer. This is why a warm glass of milk can help you sleep – sprinkle some cinnamon on it and fast forward your journey to dreamworld! Seeds, dairy, beans and lentils, sardines, almonds and rhubarb are excellent sourse of calcium.

IRON is essential for maintaining healthy energy levels. Those low in iron often suffer with fatigue, as the oxygen-carrying red blood cell shrinks without iron. Women deficient in iron have been known to have more problems sleeping than men who are deficient in it. The richest sources of iron include shellfish, spinach, liver and other offal, legumes, red meat, pumpkin seeds, quinoa, turkey and broccoli.

MAGNESIUM has been found to reduce symptoms of insomnia as it encourages relaxation. Further to this, it has also been found to reduce the amount of cortisol (stress hormone) in the body, which is a common reason for a sleepless night. Deficiency in the nutrient also leads to insomnia and the inability to remain asleep. Magnesium is also important for the absorption of calcium. It can be found in dark chocolate, avocado, nuts, legumes, tofu, seeds, salmon, wholegrains, mackerel and bananas.

ZINC is required by hundreds of enzymes in the body. Without it they would suffer, which could lead to a less effective metabolism and immune system and could contribute to unrestful sleep and fatigue. If that wasn't enough, when paired with vitamin B6, zinc has been known to increase the vividness of dreams. Rich sources of zinc include red meat, shellfish, seeds, cashews, pine nuts, almonds, dairy and dark chocolate.

MINT

....

(MENTHA)

THIS HERB IS THOUGHT TO BE THE MOST
CALMING AND SOOTHING – PERFECT FOR
A GOOD NIGHT'S SLEEP.

ORIGIN OF THE SPICE AND HISTORY

Mint is believed to have originated in the Mediterranean and Asia, and it can grow in all regions of the world where there is water. It was discovered in Egyptian tombs from over 3,000 years ago. Some of the early uses of mint included the treatment of stomach and chest pains, as well as a variety of digestive disorders.

The Greeks used mint in baths to stimulate their bodies. They were also known to use mint to clean their banqueting tables and to decorate their great halls – this may have been one of the earliest uses of mint as an air freshener. The Romans preferred to use it as an oral cleanser and a digestive aid. Some have also suggested that they used it in some of their sauces.

During Medieval times, mint was one of the herbs that was often grown in monasteries. Monks were known to use it for cooking and as a medicine. At this time the Scottish would flavour their whisky with mint, which proved popular.

Mint is still commonly used outside the kitchen, particularly for oral hygiene and in aromatherapy.

FOLKLORE

As a herb that was once offered to guests as a symbol of hospitality and friendship, mint has had a significant place in several cultures throughout history. Greek mythology stated that mint had once been a beautiful river nymph named Minthe, who was turned into a plant by Persephone, the wife of Hades. Persephone had discovered that Hades was in love with Minthe, and so she cursed her to become a plant, so that all would tread upon and crush her. After Hades failed to undo the spell, he blessed Minthe with the overwhelming aroma mint now has, so that he could smell and be near to whenever someone trod on her and released the aroma.

It is said that when the pilgrims first went to America, they took spearmint with them. This was reported by an English traveller in the seventeenth century, who noted the various herbs growing in a colony he visited in New England.

HOLISTIC BENEFITS OF MINT

One of the most common uses of mint today is as an **oral health** aid, because of its germicidal qualities. Not only is mint found in chewing gum, toothpaste and mouthwashes, but chewing it can also cleanse the mouth of harmful bacteria.

As well as being a fantastic palate cleanser, mint is beneficial to **digestive health**. By soothing the stomach and reducing inflammation, it can eliminate indigestion and flatulence while promoting healthy digestion in the gut by helping food to pass through the stomach more quickly. The aroma released when mint is chewed also promotes the secretion of enzymes in the mouth, as the salivary glands respond to the herb. This also makes mint great for weight loss, as it promotes the breakdown of food and fats by increasing the number of digestive enzymes released during meals. The menthol in mint is believed to relax the muscles of the digestive tract and alleviate symptoms of IBS.

Not only can mint help those suffering from nausea and motion sickness by calming the stomach, it can be used to **relieve pain from migraines and headaches,** too. The scent of mint is thought to be calming for the mind and can offer relief from inflammation as well as lowering temperature. These effects are intensified when mint oil is used directly on the head and temples, but crushing the leaves and inhaling the aroma also produces results.

It has been suggested that the aroma of mint can activate parts of the brain that **increase cognition and brain function**. Smelling mint has been linked with reductions in stress irritability, anxiety and depression, as well as increased energy levels.

Mint may be useful for those suffering with colds and flu. Menthol is an active ingredient in several cold and flu medicines and has been known to **improve nasal breathing**. The cooling properties of mint also aid in lowering body temperature during fevers.

NUTRITIONAL VALUE

Mint contains a healthy amount of vitamin A, iron, calcium and manganese. It also contains vitamin C, B-complex vitamins including vitamin B9 and calcium, copper, magnesium, phosphorus, potassium and zinc.

PARSLEY

....

(PETROSELINUM CRISPUM)

THIS HERB IS OFTEN A LEAFY GARNISH THAT
GETS LEFT ON THE SIDE OF THE PLATE AND
NOT EATEN, BUT THERE ARE HUGE BENEFITS
TO ADDING IT TO YOUR DIET.

ORIGIN OF THE SPICE AND HISTORY

Parsley is native to the Mediterranean, particularly the part from Southern Europe to the Balkan Peninsula. The Greeks are thought to have used parsley as a medication since prehistoric times. Hippocrates believed that it was useful for the treatment of kidney pains and rheumatism. He also claimed that it was good as a preventative medicine, which could help maintain good general health.

The ancient Greeks and Romans used parsley, but not as a food. They believed that it had some links with death, and would only grow it outside the home. It was used to line their garden borders and fed to their horses to improve their strength. Due to its associations with death, parsley was also widely used in funerals. Wreaths of parsley would be placed on tombs and the leaves would also be used to neutralise the smell of corpses.

It was not until the ninth century, when the Holy Roman Emperor decided to grow the herb in his Imperial Gardens for the purpose of cooking, that parsley began to to be eaten. Whether fresh or dried, it is now widely used in the kitchen. Today, it is often used in dishes containing tomatoes or fish, as well as in salads and soups.

FOLKLORE

The word parsley is said to have originated from the word *'petroselini'* which means rock celery, due to the fact that it was known to flourish among rocks and walls.

The Greeks and Romans preferred to not consume parsley, due to its many links with death and its association with evil. Various cultures shared these views through tales of mythology, superstition and folklore.

Greek mythology tells of an infant child named Opheltes, who was killed by snakes when left alone by his nurse; parsley was said to have grown from his wounds as the blood escaped. The Greeks then changed his name to Archemorus so that he would be known as the 'forerunner of death'. From this time, the Greeks saw parsley as an evil herb and dedicated it to Persephone, who was the goddess of spring and the partner of Hades, god of the underworld.

The Germans and the Americans believed for a time that if parsley failed to grow in a garden, it was a portent that someone in that house would die very soon.

HOLISTIC BENEFITS OF PARSLEY

As an old cure-all, parsley has long been used as a medication. It aids digestion by promoting **digestive fluid secretion** and bile production, which helps with the breakdown of foods in the gut. This herb also has the potential to relieve the symptoms of constipation, indigestion, nausea, acid reflux and flatulence. Eating parsley can also freshen the breath and cleanse the mouth.

When trying to lose weight, parsley should be on your list of essential aids. As a **natural diuretic**, it can help those who suffer from bloating, water retention, urinary tract infections, gallbladder stones and kidney stones. Parsley also **cleanses the intestinal tract,** enhancing the absorption of nutrients, which is essential for optimal health. It can also increase metabolism. The flavonoids in parsley also play a role in detoxifying the body of various harmful substances, including heavy metals. The iron in parsley will not only **cure and prevent anaemia**, but it may also give you a little boost of energy. This herb can also assist you in sleep and has been used to treat insomnia by regulating cardiac rhythms.

Vitamin C and beta-carotene make parsley a great **natural anti-inflammatory**, which is excellent for reducing aches and pains.

Having a good level of vitamin B9 (folic acid) is essential for a **healthy pregnancy** and for the development of a child in the womb. Deficiency in this vitamin can lead to birth complications, miscarriage and birth defects.

Not only can parsley reduce blemishes and scars on the skin, but the vitamins and minerals in it make it great for the maintenance of healthy skin. The herb has been known to **reduce acne,** due to its ability to maintain a healthy production of oils.

Parsley is particularly effective for **pain and wound management**. The vitamins present in it help to heal wounds and bruises while reducing pain.

Parsley has been known to help **balance hormones**, particularly in women. As well as boosting oestrogen secretion and increasing libido, it can also help those women who suffer with premenstrual syndrome (PMS) and the menopause. Vitamin K, which is found in parsley, can also help with excessive bleeding as it **aids in blood clotting**. Paired with the pain relief and antispasmodic relief offered by parsley, the herb should be on every woman's spice rack.

Bone health can be enhanced by the various vitamins and minerals in parsley. Not only do they prevent osteoporosis, deterioration and breakdown of bones, they can also increase the strength and density of bones.

The carotenoid and vitamin A present in parsley can help **protect against poor eye health** and premature degeneration, including cataracts and night vision.

NUTRITIONAL VALUE

Parsley is a nutrient-dense herb, but it is particularly rich in vitamin K. It also a good source of fibre as well as containing vitamins A, C, B2, B3 and B9, manganese, calcium, magnesium and iron.

SUMAC

······································

(RHUS)

AS WELL AS BEING A VERSATILE SPICE THAT
ADDS A TANGY LEMON FLAVOUR TO FOOD,
SUMAC IS ALSO BRILLIANT FOR
YOUR OVERALL HEALTH.

ORIGIN OF THE SPICE AND HISTORY

Sumac is known to grow in subtropical parts of the world. Of the several different species of sumac, most are native to various parts of America. One exception is Sicilian sumac, which is native to Southern Europe.

Early Greek writers discussed the use of sumac as a tanning solution to colour hides and dye silk and wool, as well as a medicine. Some of the early medicinal uses of sumac include its effectiveness for healing bruises and wounds. It was also documented as a natural painkiller and an antispasmodic. The Romans used sumac to sour their foods, as lemons were relatively unknown in Europe at that time. This practice continues today – many people in the Middle East still use it as a zesty alternative to lemon.

Sumac is popular among Lebanese, Turkish, Iranian and Syrian cuisines. It is often used to spice meats and fish, but it is also used on salads and vegetables, including aubergines and potatoes. For best use, people often sprinkle it on food just before serving, rather than cooking with it.

FOLKLORE

The word sumac is thought to have originated from the Greek word for 'red'. Some Native American tribes believed that it had the ability to predict the weather and change the seasons.

Sumac has been used to treat an astounding number of ailments over the ages. It has been thought to heal everything from colds and fevers to bladder inflammation and rectal bleeding.

For a time, it was believed that eating the berries of a sumac tree would cure those who suffer from bedwetting. This may have been because it was thought to cure several urinary problems including painful urination and urine retention.

HOLISTIC BENEFITS OF SUMAC

The **antioxidant properties** of sumac are some of the strongest of any ingredient and almost certainly highest of any herb or spice. This makes it exceptionally good for the maintenance of good health.

As a **digestive aid**, sumac is thought to improve the health of the gut in several ways and also to reduce the effects of a poor digestive system. The tannins and acids in sumac make the spice antibacterial and antifungal, which can also help with the treatment of various ailments, including **yeast infections** and **athlete's foot**. When chewed, the sumac berries can help cleanse the mouth.

The high amounts of vitamin C and gallic acid found in sumac make it great for boosting the immune system. Doctors around the globe agree that keeping vitamin C in your blood is an ideal way to maintain overall health, as it essential for the maintenance of a **healthy immune system** but may also help prevent heart failure and stroke. The nutrients in sumac assist in keeping the skin firm and young-looking by promoting collagen and maintaining the natural elasticity of the skin.

Sumac is great for **weight loss**: it has the ability to promote fat burning and has been likened to the effects of weight-loss medication.

The iron in in sumac is a great energy leveller and it is essential for the **recovery of anaemia and fatigue**. It also helps in the transportation of blood around the body and promotes healthy red blood cell formation. Sumac also contains compounds that assist in the regulation of blood sugar, and can help in the management and prevention of Type 2 diabetes and those suffering with Type 1 diabetes when used alongside their medication.

NUTRITIONAL VALUE

Sumac is a great source of vitamin A and iron. It also contains calcium and fibre.

STRESS AND MIGRAINES

Put your feet up and let's talk a little about headspace. For years, people have associated stress with ill health, and there's an abundance of evidence to back this up. Everything from heart disease to cancer has been linked with stressful lifestyles and high levels of stress hormones. Though some people are more resilient to stress than others, we will all have significant stressors throughout our lives that will cause physiological and behavioural changes in us. Imagine going on a first date, and saying, when asked about yourself, 'Hi, here's a little about me; I'm really cranky, I'm losing my sense of humour, my interest in life in dwindling, I snap at people all the time, I can never finish a task before I move on to the next, I have difficulty sleeping and I hate mornings because I have to do it all again'. Chances are, you wouldn't get a second date, but whether we say those things or not, if we let stress get the better of us, that is the person we are. Managing stress allows us to be the person we want to be, and not the monster it turns us into.

Recent evidence suggests that our negative perception of stress can be more harmful than the stress itself. Technically this should be good news, as it means that if we see stressors as challenges, we can avoid the harmful effects of feeling stressed out. Of course, this is easier said than done, and if our bodies are not equipped with the right substances to allow the body to remove the stress hormones and increase the feel-good hormones, we will have less chance of success. When our heads aren't clear, we often make poor choices, and this includes poor food choices. This is why it is essential that we give our bodies the best chance of defeating stress by fortifying it with nutrients that are known to do so. Furthermore, migraine headaches are one of the most common side effects of chronic stress and have even been known to start instantly in extreme situations. The herbs and spices used to reduce stress will make the body more resilient to migraines and general pain management. By taking control of our nutrition, we can supply the brain and body with the best defence against the things we can't control.

Let's not forget that the stress response is a naturally evolved mechanism that is designed to help us survive and succeed. Whether it's stopping us from being eaten by a lion or helping us push ourselves to meet a deadline at work, it is essential for success. The modern lifestyle disrupts the evolved stress response by keeping the stress hormones on tap, which is what leads to many of the detrimental health conditions associated with stress. This is why we should step back and take a little more care of ourselves, book a spa day or perhaps get outdoors and see some nature. It can also be quite beneficial to clear your mind. Managing stress is not easy, but if the body is not nourished in a way to deal with it as best as possible, our chance of success will be much lower.

ESSENTIAL VITAMINS AND MINERALS

VITAMIN A can help the body in its battle with stress, due to its antioxidant abilities. Foods rich in vitamin A include carrots, sweet potatoes, winter squash, apricots, spinach and kale.

B-COMPLEX vitamins have various benefits for those suffering with stress, and have often been called the 'anti-stress vitamins'. Vitamin B1 is important for the body's ability to deal with stress. Vitamin B5 is essential for the production of several stress hormones and facilitates a healthy stress response. Serotonin production and noradrenaline production are linked with high levels of the vitamin B6. Vitamins B2 and B12 have been known to reduce the frequency of migraines and vitamin B12 may also combat the emotional effects of stress. As a natural mood enhancer, it has been known to reduce levels of anxiety. Rich sources of B vitamins include poultry, fish and nuts.

VITAMIN C can help reduce stress by raising progesterone and lowering cortisol and corticosterone. Furthermore, as an antioxidant, vitamin C helps protect the cells from the harmful effects of stress. Vitamin C is also essential for the healthy functioning of the immune system, which can be hindered by stress. Low levels of vitamin C are associated with higher levels of anxiety and depression, which both lead to stress. Excellent sources include citrus fruit, mango, papaya, watermelon, strawberries, green and red cabbage, broccoli and tomatoes.

MAGNESIUM is important for the regulation of the stress response. Low levels of magnesium have been known to lead to irritability and anxiety as well as to a predisposition to stress. Magnesium deficiency has also been linked with migraines. This may be due to several factors, as magnesium contributes to healthy blood pressure, blood sugar and also to the functioning of the nervous system. Magnesium has been known to play a part in relaxation. It can be found in dark chocolate, avocado, nuts, legumes, tofu, seeds, salmon, wholegrains, mackerel and bananas.

ZINC is important for healthy adrenal activity. It is essential for fighting the negative effects of stress. Rich sources of zinc include red meat, shellfish, seeds, cashews, pine nuts, almonds, dairy, dark chocolate and wholegrains.

CARDAMOM

(ELETTARIA CARDAMOMUM)

THIS SPICE IS LOADED WITH HEALTH
BENEFITS AND IS KNOWN AS
'THE AROMATIC SPICE'.

ORIGIN OF THE SPICE AND HISTORY

Cardamom is native to India – it has been farmed there for at least 4,000 years, making it one of the world's oldest spices. It grew in such abundance that the area where it was first farmed in southern India became known as the Cardamom Hills.

Oneof the earliest uses of the spice was by the ancient Egyptians, who used it as a medicine and embalming tool, as well as during rituals. They also chewed it for its benefits to oral health.

Cardamom is used in many Middle Eastern dishes, including curries, and has also been used there for many years to make cardamom tea. It is also found in most Middle Eastern spice blends.

The Scandinavians are also famous for their use of cardamom, in both sweet and savoury dishes and in some of their alcoholic beverages. During the holiday season, cardamom has become a traditional Scandinavian flavour in food such as *krumkake* and the traditional holiday drink, *glögg*.

FOLKLORE

Cardamom has long been been used in Hindu funeral rituals when mourners pay their respects to the deceased.

In India, cardamom was used during ancient times as a digestive aid and as a cure to obesity. Other health qualities attributed to it by the old world included fortifying the liver, and nervous tissue, strengthening the stomach and as an anti-nausea medication.

The Arabs believed that cardamom was more than just a digestive aid and also prescribed it as an aphrodisiac for those with a low sex drive. It featured in *Arabian Nights* for its suggested aphrodisiac qualities.

HOLISTIC BENEFITS OF CARDAMOM

Studies have identified the consumption of cardamom as a way of **preventing cardiovascular disease**. The micronutrients in it are believed to reduce the abundance of fats in the body and help control regular heartbeat. The reduction of these harmful fats can also stimulate metabolism and aid weight loss. Cardamom has also been shown to reduce harmful cholesterol in the blood. In addition, there is evidence that the manganese in it can regulate blood sugar levels, which may assist in the prevention and management of Type 2 diabetes and may also assist with weight loss.

There is much association between cardamom and **oral health**. The antimicrobial properties in cardamom make it effective for killing bacteria in the mouth and also aid in freshening breath caused by poor oral health.

Cardamom has also been shown to help in the **digestive system**. For centuries, Chinese and Indian people have used it to aid digestion. Modern science has also confirmed that cardamom helps in several aspects of digestion and reduces the risk of gastrointestinal disorders. It has also been found to protect the stomach from ulcers. The aromatic spice can also reduce the symptoms of urinary problems, but only as a form of management rather than a cure.

The high levels of iron in cardamom make it exceptional for **reducing the risk of anaemia** and may help to reduce fatigue and assist in restful sleep. Regularly used in aromatherapy, cardamom is believed to be a natural antidepressant. When consumed as a tea, it is thought to cleanse both the body and the mind.

The manganese found in cardamom may help reduce the risk of **migraines** by removing harmful toxins from the body. Cardamom is a natural detoxifier and may also help to reduce the visible signs of ageing, such as wrinkles and dark circles under the eyes.

NUTRITIONAL VALUE

Cardamom is a fantastic source of iron and manganese. It also contains vitamin C and fibre, and magnesium, potassium, calcium and zinc.

THYME

(THYMUS VULGARIS)

THIS AROMATIC HERB HAS CULINARY
AND ORNAMENTAL USES, BUT IT ALSO HAS
MANY HEALTH BENEFITS, INCLUDING
HELPING BRONCHITIS, ARTHRITIS
AND SORE THROATS.

ORIGIN OF THE SPICE AND HISTORY

Thyme is native to the Mediterranean. Its earliest use is thought to have been as far back as 3000 BC, when the Sumerians of Mesopotamia used it as an antiseptic. Other early usage was by the Egyptians, who were known to rub it into the bodies of the deceased pharaohs as part of the embalming and mummification process. They are also thought to have burned the herb as a way of guiding the dead to the afterlife.

The Greeks also thought very highly of thyme and strongly associated it with bravery. Warriors were thought to have rubbed it on their chests before going into battle, as a way of increasing strength and bravery. It was also seen as a rite of passage for the deceased and a way of guiding warriors who fell in battle. After battles, the Greeks would mix thyme with oil and receive massages to soothe their aches and pains.

Today, thyme is commonly used to flavour meats, stews and vegetables. A number of medications, from chest rubs and cold medications to acne medication and cough syrups contain thyme, and it is also popular in toothpastes and mouthwashes because of its numerous health benefits.

FOLKLORE

The word thyme is thought to have originated from the Greek word 'thumos', which some thought to mean 'fumigate', but others have claimed meant 'bravery'.

Throughout history, thyme has been used as a symbol of bravery and courage and as a rite of passage to the afterlife. It is thought to have been used as a medication for over 5,000 years. From treating internal parasites to cough medicines and digestive aids, thyme has been one of the most consistently used herbal remedies. Today, it is still thought to cure everything from athlete's foot to haemorrhoids.

The ancient Greek warriors are thought to have mixed thyme into their drinks to enhance the intoxicating effect. They would also massage thyme oil into their bodies before battle to give them courage. It was high fashion at the time for ladies to wear thyme in their hair.

Many monasteries grew thyme and baked it in their breads. It was also thought of as protecting the monks from spoiled meat and was directly rubbed into the meat as a preservative.

HOLISTIC BENEFITS OF THYME

There is evidence that thyme is a great treatment for **respiratory disorders**. Not only can it clear the respiratory tract of phlegm and mucus, but it also relieves inflammation caused by coughing and congestion. This also makes it an effective medicine for bronchitis, colds, flu and asthma, as well as a treatment for seasonal allergies. Vitamin C is present in thyme, so the immune system is also enhanced by this herb.

With its high amount of phenolic antioxidants and nutrients, thyme is great for those trying to protect their **heart health** and their health in general. It can also reduce bad cholesterol in the blood and increase beneficial cholesterol in the blood, further decreasing the risk of heart disease.

The herb will **increase the density and strength of the bones,** as well as reducing the risk of degenerative bone disorders and bone diseases such as osteoporosis.

Thyme is a natural remedy for bad breath and promotes **good oral health**. As well as eliminating the odour, thyme actually eliminates the bacteria that cause the issue to begin with. For this reason, several antiseptic mouthwashes have thyme as their active ingredient.

Several aromatherapies recognise the benefits of thyme on mood. This herb can **reduce symptoms of depression and insomnia,** and there are even reports suggesting that it can aid restful sleep by eliminating nightmares.

Thyme is thought to be one of the best antibacterial herbs, surpassing the effectiveness of the powerhouse spices, cinnamon and clove. This makes it a natural preserver of foods and it can protect against food-borne illnesses.

NUTRITIONAL VALUE

Thyme is a nutrient-dense spice, which contains high levels of vitamin K, and C and good levels of vitamin A. The herb also contains fibre, copper, manganese, iron and vitamin B2. There are also low levels of calcium, selenium, phosphorus, potassium, zinc and the vitamins B6, B9 and E.

OREGANO

(ORIGANUM VULGARE)

THIS HERB IS GREAT IN A SALAD OR
ON A PIZZA BUT IT ALSO HAS MANY
MEDICINAL USES, INCLUDING BEING
GREAT FOR YOUR SKIN.

ORIGIN OF THE SPICE AND HISTORY

Oregano is native to the Mediterranean and East Asia. Some species of it are believed to have been cultivated in Egypt since at least 1000 BC. The Egyptians were thought to have used it as a medicine and a preservative, as well as a disinfectant. Some of the earliest evidence of the herb dates from around 1500 BC, where images of oregano were inscribed on stone tablets by the Hittites in Asia (the ancient Anatolians).

The ancient Greeks would have likely been the earliest people to have used this herb. It became common in several Greek traditions including wedding ceremonies, where wreaths of oregano would crown the couple's heads. It was also prized for its healing abilities and particularly as an antiseptic.

It is believed that oregano is the one of the largest selling culinary herbs, if not *the* largest. America is one of the biggest consumers of it and consumes an estimated 400,000 metric tons of it each year.

Oregano still has a place in modern medicine. The thymol and carvacrol contained in it have been found to loosen phlegm and ease the bronchial passages. For this reason, thymol is found in some common cough remedies. Other substances found in oregano, such as borneol, are said to aid the digestive system too. Not just a pizza topping then!

FOLKLORE

The name Origanum is said to have come from the ancient Greek word for 'mountain joy'.

Throughout history, there are several documents describing the effects of oregano, though the validity of these is always questioned as the spice has consistently been confused with the closely related marjoram. The history and folklore of each herb may refer to the other, as the two were difficult to separate.

In Greek mythology oregano was associated with Aphrodite and it was said to have grown on Mount Olympus. The Romans believed the herb was created by the god Venus who gave it a distinct scent so that mortals would be reminded of her beauty. The Greeks and Romans would crown the bride and groom with oregano during a wedding service, as the herb was thought to bring joy.

Varieties of oregano were also used in beer production, before hops became the predominant herb in beer making.

HOLISTIC BENEFITS OF OREGANO

We all get a little full from time to time, which is why it is important to choose your ingredients wisely if you're planning on having a heavy meal. Oregano is an ingredient that can actually aid **healthy digestion** so that you feel fuller for longer, while enhancing the digestive system's efficiency. Not only does the fibre promote intestinal movements and reduce the risk of constipation and diarrhoea, but it also increases appetite and reduces intestinal problems, such as cramps and even infections and parasites.

Oregano can **improve blood circulation** and **reduce harmful cholesterol**, which decreases the risk of heart attack, stroke and atherosclerosis. The potassium in oregano makes it great for maintaining a healthy blood pressure.

This Mediterranean wonder herb can also **prevent anaemia** due to its high iron content, which is essential for the production of haemoglobin. It also helps reduce fatigue and aids the maintenance of healthy energy levels, as it sends oxygen to your cells and muscles, increasing strength.

The anti-inflammatory properties of oregano have identified the herb as a natural **pain reliever**. Body aches, toothache, muscle spasms and sinus headaches are among the ailments thought to be helped by its consumption.

Menstrual cramps and discomfort caused by menstruation and the menopause have also been reduced by oregano consumption. Not only can oregano reduce the intensity of these pains but there is evidence that it may also assist in the regulation of a **healthy menstrual cycle,** and some studies even suggest that it can aid in the prevention of premature menopause.

The large amounts of vitamin K, calcium, manganese and iron in oregano make it fantastic for **bone health**. Oregano provides an astounding amount of your daily vitamin K, which not only helps to keep your bones strong but also assists in the prevention of bone disorders, including osteoporosis.

Oregano can help in **healthy ageing** by keeping your skin and hair strong and healthy. As a great antioxidant, oregano can protect cells from premature death and oxidative damage, which can lead to premature ageing. There is also evidence that the nutrients in oregano aid in the prevention of age-related mental decline and enhance brain activity, protecting the brain from conditions, such as Alzheimer's disease and dementia. This makes it an aid to healthy ageing. Millions of people in the Mediterranean who enjoy both oregano and long, healthy lives can't be wrong, can they?

NUTRITIONAL VALUE

Oregano is rich in calcium, iron, manganese and vitamin K. It also contains vitamins A and E and several of the B-complex vitamins including B1, B2, B3 and B5 as well as magnesium and potassium.

MARJORAM

. . . .

(OREGANUM MARJORANA)

THIS HERB IS ALSO KNOWN AS 'THE HAPPY
HERB', AND IS COMMONLY USED TO TREAT
COUGHS AND COLDS.

ORIGIN OF THE SPICE AND HISTORY

Marjoram is indigenous to the Middle East and the Mediterranean. Earliest evidence of it dates from around 1500 BC, when images of the herb were inscribed on stone tablets by the Hittites of Asia (the ancient Anatolians).

Marjoram was used in beer before hops became the predominant herb in beer making.

The Egyptians used marjoram oil to treat ailments such as ear infections, and also used the herb as an antiseptic. It has been used for its healing properties by many other cultures throughout history, too.

FOLKLORE

The name translates as 'Mountain Joy'. It originally referred to marjoram, but most botanists agree that back then we mistook oregano for marjoram, so the name applies to both herbs.

In Greek mythology, marjoram was associated with Aphrodite (the creator of marjoram and oregano) and was said to have grown on Mount Olympus. The Romans believed that the herb was created by the god Venus, who gave it the distinct scent so that mortals could be reminded of her beauty. The Greeks and Romans crowned the bride and groom with marjoram in wedding ceremonies, as the herb was also thought to bring joy.

In Greece marjoram was often placed on graves, as it was said that if the deceased had found a peaceful afterlife, then marjoram would grow.

The Egyptians used marjoram in their embalming practices and even wore it during rituals for their god of the afterlife, Osiris.

HOLISTIC BENEFITS OF MARJORAM

Marjoram contains carvacrol, which is **antifungal, antiviral and antiseptic**, and can inhibit the growth of many bacteria. It can also improve blood circulation and prevent anaemia due to its high iron content.

Marjoram can also **aid digestion** by increasing appetite and **reducing intestinal problems**, such as cramps, constipation, diarrhoea and even intestinal infections.

It has been linked with reducing and preventing symptoms of **cold and flu,** particularly in marjoram tea, and can also help in the treatment of asthma.

A natural anti-inflammatory, marjoram has been linked with **pain relief** and is also known to reduce body aches, toothache, muscle spasms and sinus headaches.

Relief of **anxiety, depression and stress** have all been associated with marjoram.

The large amount of vitamins and minerals in marjoram helps with the prevention and treatment of Alzheimer's disease, dementia and nerve damage. It also promotes the maintenance of a healthy heart rate and blood pressure, while enhancing brain activity.

Marjoram is **good for your bones**. The large amounts of vitamin K in it provide an astounding amount of your daily recommendation, which helps to keep your bones strong and aids in the prevention of bone disorders including osteoporosis.

Like oregano, marjoram keeps you young by **keeping your skin and hair strong and healthy**. A great antioxidant, it will also help the transportation of oxygen, giving you higher energy levels.

NUTRITIONAL VALUE

Marjoram is a rich source of vitamins K, A, C and B6 as well as calcium, iron, magnesium, copper, zinc and manganese.

WEIGHT LOSS

Balance, realistic goals and consistency is what you need. It's best that we start with the answer for this one, as some of what you read here may not tally with what you may have read in the media. There is more in the media about diet and weight loss than ever, but rather than throw the latest yoyo diet at you or tell you a way to lose weight quickly to look great for your next holiday, I thought I would slow it down and explain two simple things. Why weight loss matters, and how to achieve it responsibly for the rest of your life. Once you decide that this is for you, you will see how easy, natural and tasty weight loss can be.

Losing weight is not about going to the gym for 30 years in order to live for an extra ten, but it is about quality of life, throughout your whole life. The goal should be walking up the stairs with ease, taking long walks with friends and family without needing to take frequent breaks and not needing to go to the doctors regularly. This is preventive action taking control and becoming the best version of yourself possible, so that every day is more enjoyable, and you can live life to your true potential. Its never too late to make the change.

I started by telling you that balance, realistic goals and consistency are the way forward, and ultimately that is all you should need. Forget about the ridiculous fad diets designed to line the pockets of people who do not care for your health. Ignore the temptation to try the 'milkshake' diets that have been proven time and time again to fail at producing any lasting effect. And try to avoid fat clubs if you can (because let's face it, if they worked, they'd be out of business). They know you'll be back next year for another expensive dose of temporary and unhealthy weight loss, so let's prove them wrong.

When it comes to weight management, the most successful long-term results come from long-lasting and healthy lifestyle changes. Ultimately, if your input (food and drink consumption) is higher than your output (daily activity expenditure), you will put weight on, regardless of your genetic make-up. This is also true of weight loss. If your output is higher than your input, then you will lose weight. The problem is that losing weight is not always done in a healthy manner, and this is where balance comes in. There are certain foods, particularly herbs and spices, that have been known to aid in weight loss by helping the body break down fats in various ways. Let's be clear about one thing though – simply adding these into your diet will not make all the difference by itself. It is equally important to eliminate the foods that hinder and reduce their benefits, such as processed foods and foods that are high in saturated fat, salt and sugar. I often get asked if it is OK to eat cakes and biscuits. You can, but make them yourself without all the added toxic fats and sugars.

Herbs and spices can do a lot more than make you more creative in your cooking; they're a guilt-free way to flavour food while giving you a healthy boost of vitamins and minerals. There are so many desserts and snacks that can be made more tasty with a sprinkle of spice, which would also help you lose weight. Getting used to spices instead of sugar, and herbs instead of salt, can bring an exotic atmosphere to your kitchen. Allow yourself to enter a new style of weight loss where you eat the foods you like in moderation, and snack on foods that help you get stronger. Make a choice to be healthier.

ESSENTIAL VITAMINS AND MINERALS

B-COMPLEX VITAMINS are extremely important in aiding weight loss. Aside from maintaining a healthy metabolism, oxygenated blood and the regulation of blood sugar levels, B-complex vitamins can help the nervous system, brain functionality and cellular function in the body, which all help with weight management. Rich sources of B vitamins include poultry, fish and nuts.

VITAMIN C is important for converting glucose into energy, which would otherwise be converted into fat. It is also important for managing blood sugar and the synthesis and regulation of hormones that control our craving and appetite behaviours. Vitamin C will also help blood flow, which is essential and exceptionally important for overweight individuals. As an antioxidant, it also assists in the prevention of heart disease and some cancers, as well as boosting the body's natural immune system. Excellent sources include citrus fruit, mango, papaya, watermelon, strawberries, green and red cabbage, broccoli and tomatoes.

VITAMIN D is important for those trying to lose weight because of insulin sensitivity. A deficiency in vitamin D can also lead to the body converting sugar into fat rather than energy, and this also causes the body to store the fat, leading to weight gain. Vitamin D can help individuals eat less by making them feel fuller for longer. It also helps the immune system to function properly and aids cell development. Foods such as tuna, mackerel, cheese and egg yolks are high in vitamin D.

VITAMIN E can reduce high blood sugar levels and aid in the maintenance of healthy levels of blood sugar while increasing circulation of blood in the body. As an antioxidant, this vitamin can also stop cell damage and reduce the risk of cardiovascular disease. Good sources include sunflower seeds, almonds, hazelnuts and avocado.

CALCIUM works best with vitamin D qs a fat-burning mineral. As calcium is stored in fat cells, an increase in calcium is said to lead to fat being released from them burned into energy. Clinical trials have also found positive correlations between calcium intake and weight loss. Did you know that skimmed milk actually contains more calcium than full-fat milk? This is because the calcium is stored in the watery part of the milk. Excellent sources include dairy, seeds, beans and lentils, almonds and rhubarb.

FIBRE is important for keeping you fuller for longer. This will reduce the number of snacks you eat and also keep you feeling more satisfied after a meal. Fibre is also important for pushing food through the digestive system and assists in the uptake of nutrients. Foods rich in fibre include wholewheat pasta, wholegrain bread, oats, barley, rye, berries, pears, melon, broccoli and potatoes skins.

IRON transports oxygen to every organ in the body. It is essential for energy levels and without it, fatigue, loss of strength and even organ failure can occur. For those trying to lose weight, motivation and energy levels are key ingredients for success, so be sure to consume healthy amounts of iron. The richest sources include shellfish, spinach, liver and other offal; legumes, red meat, pumpkin seeds, quinoa, turkey and broccoli.

MAGNESIUM is important for neutralising stomach acid, which leads to healthy digestion. For those trying to keep active, magnesium also reduces the risk of muscle cramps and low energy levels, as it assists in muscle contractions and gives your energy levels a boost. It can be found in dark chocolate, avocado, nuts, legumes, tofu, seeds, salmon, wholegrains, mackerel and bananas.

MANGANESE can help with the regulation of fat metabolism and blood sugar. This can help individuals trying to lose weight by reducing their cravings for unhealthy foods. Good sources include mussels, sweet potatoes, chickpeas, spinach and pineapple.

POTASSIUM can fight against bloating and aid in muscle contractions in digestion. Potassium-rich foods include dried fruits, bananas, garlic, onions, legumes and nuts.

ZINC can help tissue regeneration after exercise and also strengthens the immune system and viral resistance. It is essential in the use of numerous enzymes, without which metabolism would suffer. Rich sources of zinc include red meat, shellfish, seeds, cashews, pine nuts, almonds, dairy, dark chocolate and wholegrains.

CINNAMON

....

(CINNAMOMUM VERUM)

THIS SPICE IS BOTH DELICIOUS AND FULL OF
MANY IMPRESSIVE HEALTH BENEFITS,
INCLUDING LOWERING BLOOD
SUGAR LEVELS AND REDUCING
HEART DISEASE.

ORIGIN OF THE SPICE AND HISTORY

Cinnamon is native to Sri Lanka and is a spice that was used as far back as 2800 BC. The signature smell is one that often evokes warm, cosy feelings in most, but the history of cinnamon is filled with war, extortion and mythology.

During the Middle Ages, cinnamon was used as a medicine to relieve coughs, colds and sore throats. This was a practice made popular by the Chinese, who in ancient times would use the spice for its healing abilities. For a time, the origin of cinnamon was a complete mystery, and people believed that the way to obtain it was through birds. Legend told of birds who would carry cinnamon sticks from an unknown land to build their nests, where Arabs would then trick them in order to acquire the sticks. This led to the creation of the mythological creature known as the cinnamon bird. Another story was that cinnamon could only be found at the bottom of deep canyons, where it was guarded by vicious snakes.

It was said that global exploration in the fifteenth and sixteenth centuries was in part driven by the search for cinnamon, as its price was so extortionate. The Portuguese and Spanish wanted to capitalise on the spice, which was commonly used to hide the scent of spoiled meat. At that time, the Italians had a monopoly on the trading of it in Europe. It was said that this was possible as Venetian traders would travel to Egypt to obtain it.

Today, cinnamon is produced in various tropical climates, which has allowed it to become an affordable spice that is still growing in popularity. It has become a modern household commodity that is used in sweet and savoury dishes, as well as being sprinkled on hot drinks.

FOLKLORE

Though many spices come from grinding fruits and berries, cinnamon comes from the peeling, drying and grinding of the cinnamon tree's bark.

Though it was an expensive spice at the time, it has been said that the Roman Emperor Nero burned an entire year's worth of cinnamon at the funeral of his wife Poppaea, as a sign of his deep mourning. However, this may have been a sign of remorse for killing his wife in the first place!

The Chinese still use cinnamon as a medicine today, but rather than using it to treat illness they take it daily as a preventative supplement. In China and India it is also used to treat menstrual pain and to promote regular menstruation.

HOLISTIC BENEFITS OF CINNAMON

Cinnamon is an effective **preventative medication**. Regular consumption of it can regulate blood pressure and lower cholesterol levels, which increases the chances of maintaining a healthy heart and prevents heart disease. The antioxidant properties in cinnamon also protect against degenerative diseases and maintain good cell health. Cinnamon is also naturally antibacterial, which makes it effective for the reduction of infection and of bacteria in the body. Paired with its warming abilities, it can aid in the treatment of colds, flu and fevers.

The anti-inflammatory properties of cinnamon are the reason for its effective use in the treatment of diseases, such as arthritis and muscle and joint pain. Cinnamon **reduces inflammation and offers pain relief**, while reducing the risk of blood clots. Magnesium present in cinnamon also strengthens bones and, combined with the calcium found in it, this spice is effective in the prevention and treatment of osteoporosis.

Cinnamon has been known to be effective in **improving the body's response to insulin,** as certain flavonoids in cinnamon can mimic the effects of it. This is important for those suffering with Type 2 diabetes and those trying to prevent it. Regular consumption of this spice lowers blood sugar levels too, and it is effective at reducing the craving for sugar. For this reason, cinnamon should be in the kitchen of anyone hoping to maintain healthy weight management or to enhance their weight-loss programme.

Several components of cinnamon make it effective for the stimulation and promotion of a **healthy digestive system**. Fibre in cinnamon makes it effective in keeping the digestive muscles healthy and active. It can also assist in the relief of constipation and diarrhoea.

Some evidence suggests that merely sniffing cinnamon can give the brain a little boost. This has been tested with various cognitive activities and improvements in attention, concentration and working memory have all been linked to cinnamon. There is also some evidence that cinnamon promotes the creation of new neural pathways, which can aid those in the ageing population.

NUTRITIONAL VALUE

Cinnamon is a good source of calcium, iron, manganese and vitamin K. It also contains some B-complex vitamins, including vitamins B3 and B6, as well as vitamin E, magnesium, copper, potassium and zinc.

GARLIC

·····································

(ALLIUM SATIVUM)

THIS IS USED FOR MANY CONDITIONS
RELATING TO THE HEART AND BLOOD SYSTEM,
INCLUDING HIGH BLOOD PRESSURE AND HIGH
CHOLESTEROL. IT IS SOMETIMES REFERRED TO AS
'A ROSE BY ANY OTHER NAME'.

ORIGIN OF THE SPICE AND HISTORY

Though there is no agreement on the origin of garlic, it is suggested that the plant was native to either Central Asia or Northeast Iran, though some suggest that it is native to Siberia. What is generally agreed on is that garlic has been used for over 5,000 years as a medicine, a food and even a currency.

Early records indicate that the Egyptians worshipped garlic and even made clay idols of garlic bulbs, which were placed in the tombs of the fallen pharaohs. It is also thought that the workers who built the pyramids were fed garlic to help them in their laborious jobs and were given it as a form of payment. During the building of the pyramids, a shortage of garlic is said to be the reason for one of the only two times that the slaves revolted and refused to work. This shortage was said to have been caused by a flood in the Nile.

Throughout history, garlic has been mentioned in medical and religious texts, where it is praised for its medicinal benefits. There have been claims that garlic has the ability to prevent illnesses, including heart disease. There have also been claims that it can provide energy, prolong life and even enhance sexual appetite.

Garlic has always been a staple in the Mediterranean, but the popular ingredient is now used in many cuisines all over the globe, including Asian, African, European and American foods.

FOLKLORE

It simply wouldn't be possible to write about the folklore around garlic without mentioning vampires, so here we go! Throughout the ages and before it had been popularised by television and movies, garlic was thought to contain evil-repelling properties, though this was not exclusive to the evil of werewolves and vampires. Garlic was placed above doors in order to ward away the evil eye, wicked witches, the horns of a bull and even the black plague. It was also once thought that garlic had the power to keep jealous nymphs away from pregnant ladies and engaged maidens. One religious text even claimed that garlic grew in the footprints of Satan as he left the Garden of Eden.

Garlic was seen as a 'passion herb' by the Tibetan monks who banned it and also warned that widows and adolescents should steer clear of the desire-inducing ingredient. Chinese doctors often prescribed it to those suffering from problems with intimacy and low libido. It was rumoured that unfaithful husbands would chew garlic to hide the scent of their lovers as they returned home to their wives. Groomsmen have also been known to wear garlic in their buttonholes to encourage sexual activity on their wedding night.

HOLISTIC BENEFITS OF GARLIC

The allicin found in garlic is responsible for its pungent scent, but it is also the reason behind its abundance of health benefits. One of the common uses of garlic in modern medicine is the **control of hypertension**. As a natural vasodilator, garlic can reduce blood pressure and the risk of various heart disease associated with hypertension. Raw garlic can also reduce blood sugar levels and aid those suffering from or attempting to prevent diabetes. Garlic also improves blood circulation and lowers the levels of cholesterol that build up in the veins and arteries, which makes it fantastic in the prevention and treatment of various heart diseases as well as stroke and atherosclerosis.

The increase in blood flow and vasodilation that comes from eating garlic is said to be responsible for its association with **increased sexual appetite**. Garlic has been known to promote healthy blood flow to the sexual organs in both men and women, which also leads to increased libido.

The vitamins and minerals in garlic make it an effective natural anti-inflammatory and antioxidant, which can **alleviate joint pain** and reduce the risk of rheumatoid arthritis. Compounds found in garlic can also protect against cartilage damage, further protecting your joints. These properties also make garlic effective in the **prevention of neurodegenerative disorders**, such as dementia and Alzheimer's disease.

Garlic is also known to be a great **digestive aid**. As well as promoting healthy blood flow, it can assist the stomach in its functionality by stimulating the internal muscles to secrete the gastric juices that help digestion. The antibacterial properties of garlic also assist in destroying the parasites that can cause peptic ulcers.

For anyone who suffers with a poor immune system, garlic is a must. **Mineral absorption** is enhanced by garlic, which makes all other immune-boosting foods more effective. The vitamins and minerals found in garlic including vitamin C and manganese further enhance the strength of the body's **ability to fight illness and disease**. The antibacterial and antiviral properties also make it effective for the relief of colds, coughs and other respiratory conditions. As a natural expectorant, it is useful for those who suffer from bronchitis.

Garlic is great for **bone health** and can **increase oestrogen levels** in menopausal women, which aids in the prevention of osteoarthritis. It also reduces the risk of bone deterioration while strengthening bone density.

The antifungal properties of garlic have long been associated with **treatment of various fungal infections,** including ringworm and athlete's foot. Garlic has also been known to offer relief to women who suffer with yeast infections.

NUTRITIONAL VALUE

Garlic is packed with nutrients, including vitamins C and B6 and manganese. It also contains other B-complex vitamins, calcium, phosphorus, selenium, copper and zinc.

ALLSPICE

·····································

(PIMENTA DIOICA)

THIS SPICE IS KNOWN AS AN 'ALL-CURE',
AS IT IS RICH IN ANTIOXIDANT AND
ANTI-INFLAMMATORY AGENTS.

ORIGIN OF THE SPICE AND HISTORY

Allspice is believed to have originated in the West Indies in the Caribbean. It is also native to parts of America.

Allspice is said to hace been used by the Mayan Indians, who are thought to have embalmed the bodies of their deceased leaders in it. The Arawak Indian tribes are also said to have used it as a food preservative and as a way of curing meat.

Allspice is a particularly fussy spice that prefers the Caribbean climate to other parts of the world; several countries including India and the famous 'spice islands' have been unsuccessful in their attempts to cultivate it.

Other early uses of allspice include the pickling of fish when used as a whole berry, or ground up into a powder and used in cakes.

Today, allspice is still used medicinally. It can be found in some toothpastes, and dentists also harness the eugenol found in it to kill bacteria on the teeth and gums. In the Caribbean, allspice is still indispensable and is used to flavour many dishes, including seafood and Creole sausages. It is also one of the key components of jerk seasoning. Allspice is also used in many desserts in various parts of the world, including Christmas pudding.

FOLKLORE

Allspice is actually a berry, and when cultivated as an oil, it has been known to lift the spirit and increase one's self-confidence. These effects are thought to be especially prevalent when allspice is added to tea.

Throughout history, allspice has been used as a medication for pain management. Relief of toothache and inflammation in the body are among some of its benefits.

The healing effects of allspice were first observed when the berry was added to bath water, which would bring about temporary pain relief. It would also induce a mild anaesthetic effect on the bather.

The smoking of allspice berries in Jamaica in not uncommon. A long pipe is needed to enjoy allspice in this way, but the Jamaicans speak highly about its use as an alternative to tobacco.

Now a popular Christmas spice, allspice is ideal for the times when we eat extremely heavy meals, as it has several properties that aid digestion. It has also been used to increase appetite as well as improving oral health. More cake, anyone?

HOLISTIC BENEFITS OF ALLSPICE

Allspice has a multitude of health benefits. It is most beneficial for **preventing ill health**, which is due to the fact that the spice has anti-inflammatory, antiseptic, antioxidant, antibacterial, antifungal and antimicrobial properties. These factors make allspice a modern-day cure-all and an amazing way to slow the effects of ageing, including the reduction of wrinkles and age spots.

The various minerals found in allspice make it a **fantastic aid for the digestive system**. Adding this spice to your meals could help reduce flatulence while also regulating bowel movements and lowering the risk of constipation and diarrhoea. It is also known to reduce stomach cramps and increase appetite as well as to reduce nausea and vomiting. The manganese present in this spice can help in weight loss, as it regulates fat metabolism and blood glucose.

The **antibacterial, antimicrobial and antiseptic properties** of this spice make it fantastic for dental health.

The iron contained in allspice can help those suffering with **fatigue** or anyone who needs an **energy boost** – low levels of iron can make you irritable and easily distracted, which can lead to stress and depression.

The ability to **regulate blood pressure** and **improve the immune system fuctionality** make allspice essential for cardiovascular health. The magnesium and calcium in it also contribute towards healthy functionality of the arteries, further reducing the risk of cardiovascular disease.

Allspice is also said to help those who suffer with **heavy menstrual bleeding** and the associated pains of menstruation.

NUTRITIONAL VALUE

Allspice contains a good amount of manganese and a fair quantity of calcium, magnesium iron and fibre. It also contains vitamins C and B3.

SPICE
FOR BEAUTY

Spices aren't just key to how we feel – they can also enhance how we look after ourselves physically. As well as trying to consume as much spice as I can in my daily diet, it is also at the centre of my beauty regime – I try to use as much as possible on my skin and hair. I love nothing more than making up a treatment to put on my face after a long day – it's the perfect way to relax and keep glowing.
Hair treatments, homemade face tonics and body scrubs – your humble spices can be used to create them all.

BEFORE YOU GET STARTED

◊ Most recipes in this beauty section require cups. A classic English teacup is perfect.

◊ With all the skin treatments in this section it is advisable to do a patch test
24 hours before application.

ALLSPICE

USES

◊ One or two drops of allspice oil directly applied to an aching tooth can relieve pain.
Alternatively, it can be diluted in water to make a natural herbal mouthwash.

◊ Whether whole or ground, allspice can be boiled in an after-meal tea to ease digestion.

ALLSPICE MOUTHWASH

1 cup boiling water
1 tbsp rosemary needles
2 tsp allspice berries
1 tsp honey

1. Boil the water.

2. Pour the water into a mug and find a tea infuser or something
to put your rosemary and allspice in. Steep for 5 minutes.

3. Remove the infuser, add the honey (if using) and stir
until dissolved.

ANISE

USES

◊ The oil and tannins in anise seeds can tighten the muscles
and soothe the skin, making it healthy and gorgeous.

◊ Anise is brilliant for gripes – I gave a diluted version to my babies when
they had colic, and it really helped.

◊ This also makes a wonderfully soothing tea if you have a bad tummy.

ANISE TEA AND TONER

1 glass water
2–3 anise seeds

1. Boil the water and anise seeds together to make a tea.

2. Cool it in a jar, then use every morning to wash your face with.

BASIL

USES

◊ Basil leaves are full of potent anti-itch compounds called camphene and thymol that relieve skin irritations, prickly heat, itching and infections. The essential oils present in basil leaves have powerful antibiotic, antibacterial, disinfectant and antifungal properties that can treat various kinds of skin diseases, ringworm and itchiness caused by psoriasis, sunburn, insect bites and allergies.

◊ The natural oils and antioxidants present in basil make it an effective remedy for naturally glowing skin. Urusolic acid helps tone the skin, closing the open pores and cleaning excess oil, dirt and dead skin cells from the skin surface to give it a brighter, cleaner and fairer appearance.

◊ Another important aspect of basil in improving complexion lies in its natural detoxifying power, which relieves the skin from the effects of pollution, ultraviolet rays, stress and infection which cause microbes and viruses.

Crush a handful of basil leaves along with the roots of the plant, and apply to the affected skin. Leave for an hour and wash off with water. This should be repeated twice a day for best results.

Or

Boil a handful of basil and neem leaves in 500ml water, strain, cool and apply to the affected skin using a piece of clean cotton. Store the remaining water in the freezer and apply it twice a day.

Or

Crush a handful of basil leaves and turn it into a thick paste. Add 1 tbsp each of sandalwood powder and lemon juice and mix well. Apply to your face, leave for 1 hour, and then wash off with water. Repeat three times a week for best results.

CACAO

USES

◇ Raw cacao is very high in antioxidants that block harmful free radicals in the body, which cause inflammation and wrinkles.

◇ Cacao also contains a good amount of vitamin C and magnesium, which helps to protect the skin and keep it healthy.

ANTIOXIDANT FACE MASK

1 tbsp raw cacao powder

2 tsp clay, such as Moroccan red clay

½ tsp oil (I use jojoba oil)

1 small mug of steeped and cooled green tea

1. Mix the dry ingredients together in a small bowl.

2. Add the oil to the dry ingredients and then add the cooled green tea 1 tsp at a time, until a creamy, pudding-like consistency is reached.

3. Apply in a thick layer over your face and leave for 10–15 minutes.

4. Use an old facecloth (the mask will stain fabric) to remove the mask by holding the cloth under hot running water, squeezing it out and holding it to your face, to give it some steam and warm it up. Make sure it is not too hot though, as you don't want to scald your face.

5. Gently wipe the mask off. Follow with a cool water rinse, pat dry and then apply a few drops of your favourite facial oil (I like jojoba and neroli).

CHAMOMILE

USES

◇ Chamomile is commonly used to help calm people: it has been shown that it can be effective in aiding relaxation and helping with anxiety, depression and insomnia.

◇ If used on a regular basis, chamomile tea nourishes and moisturises your skin.

APPLE CHAMOMILE TEA

3–4 tbsp fresh chamomile flowers (If you don't have access to flowers then use 1 teabag of 100% chamomile tea)

1 apple, cut into small slices

1 cup boiling water

honey (optional)

1. Rinse the flowers with cool water.

2. Warm a teapot with boiling water.

3. Add the apple slices to the pot.

4. Add the chamomile flowers and pour in the boiling water.

5. Cover and steep for 3–5 minutes.

6. Strain the tea and add honey to taste.

SKINCARE

With any leftover chamomile tea, leave to cool and then soak a wash cloth in it, before applying to your face for 5–15 minutes. Your skin should feel soft and ready for sleep.

Placing cooled-down chamomile tea bags under the eyes can help reduce under-eye dark circles and puffiness. It also soothes tired eyes.

CARDAMOM

USES

◊   A mixture of cardamom, cinnamon and black pepper can work wonders for treating a sore throat. Cardamom soothes the throat and reduces irritation, while cinnamon offers antibacterial protection and black pepper improves the bio availability of both ingredients.

◊   Cardamom has also been found to reduce nausea and prevent vomiting. In one study, test subjects who were given ground cardamom showed less frequent nausea and vomiting.

◊   Chewing on seeds freshens your breath.

◊   If you are trying to prevent cigarette cravings, cardamom has anecdotally been shown to combat the symptoms.

◊   The antioxidants in cardamom can promote heart health. It also contains fibre, which can help to lower cholesterol levels.

◊   Cardamom is great for your skin, due to its antibacterial and antioxidant properties. It can be used to cleanse the skin as well as improve complexion and help treat skin allergies.

CARDAMOM ROSE MASK

a pinch of ground cardamom
1 cup rose water
¾ cups rolled oats

1. Mix all the ingredients together well.

2. Apply on damp, make-up free skin and leave on for 5 minutes.

3. Wash off with a warm flannel.

CHILLI/CAYENNE

USES

◊ Chilli is rich in beta-carotene, capsaicin and vitamins A and C, powerful antioxidants that help to stimulate new cell growth and repair skin.

◊ Chilli is a natural stimulant and helps fight ageing in your skin.

◊ Capsaicin blocks sun-damaging factors from activating.

CAYENNE PEPPER MASK

1 tsp raw cacao powder

½ tsp cayenne pepper
(¼ tsp for sensitive skin)

half an avocado

1. Mix the cacao and cayenne pepper together, add the avocado and blend until smooth.

2. Apply to the face. Leave for 5–10 minutes and then wash off.

COCONUT-CHILLI MASK

2 tbsp coconut oil

½ tsp lemon juice

1 tsp honey

1 tbsp ground coffee

½ tsp chilli flakes

½ tsp ground cinnamon

1. Mix all the ingredients together in a bowl until smooth.

2. Apply to the face. Leave for 5–10 minutes and then wash off.

CINNAMON

USES

◊ Cinnamon can be used to prevent hair loss and achieve hair growth because of its ability to exfoliate.

◊ It also helps to remove build up from the scalp, causing healthier hair follicles that then promote better hair growth.

◊ It causes a tingling sensation when applied, which is thought to draw blood to the scalp for stimulation.

◊ Cinnamon is also known to help remove sunspots from the skin.

HAIR PASTE

1 tbsp ground cinnamon
¼ tsp warm olive oil
1 tbsp honey

1. Mix all the ingredients together.

2. Massage into the scalp, leave on for 15 minutes and then rinse.

FACE SCRUB

1 tsp ground cinnamon
1 tsp sugar
1 tbsp honey

1. Mix all the ingredients together.

2. Apply to the face, scrubbing gently, then rinse.

CLOVES

USES

◊ For centuries, clove tea has been used to soothe abdominal pain. It has analgesic qualities that work well for those suffering from gas pain or other stomach upsets.

◊ Clove tea has been used to kill intestinal parasites and also kills bacteria and fungus infections, such as oral thrush.

◊ Cloves stimulate blood flow, saliva production and gastric secretions to aid in digestion. In addition, it has anti-emetic (anti-nausea) effects.

◊ Clove oil is also known to relieve tooth pain.

ENGLISH TEA WITH CLOVES

1 English breakfast teabag
1 cup boiling water
1 tsp cloves

1. Make a cup of English breakfast tea as normal and add the cloves.

2. Drink the tea black or with milk.

SKIN

3 drops clove oil
2 tsp honey

1. Mix the clove oil and honey together.

2. Apply to the face and then rinse.

CORIANDER

USES

◇ Coriander is extremely rich in folate, antioxidants, vitamin C and beta-carotene. Your skin feels soft, supple and glowing when your cells are protected from oxidative stress.

FACE MASKS

CORIANDER WITH ALOE VERA: Freshly ground coriander in combination with aloe vera can be applied to the skin, which helps delay the onset of wrinkles and reduces fine lines.

CORIANDER WITH LEMON JUICE: A combination of ground coriander with lemon juice, when applied on the affected area, can do wonders for acne and blackheads. Coriander enables the dead cells to be removed and leads to rejuvenated skin.

CORIANDER FACE PACK: Grind the coriander, add milk, honey and lemon juice and apply to the face. This face pack will leave you with glowing skin.

CORIANDER WITH RICE AND YOGURT: A combination of ground rice and yogurt relaxes facial muscles and cells, leaving you refreshed. Make a mixture of it and apply it like a mask.

CUMIN

USES

◊ Our hair is composed of fat, water, protein and carbohydrates and we need to replenish these in order to promote proper hair growth. Black cumin contains more than 100 nutrients and vitamins that will replenish your hair.

HAIR RINSE

1½ tsp black cumin seeds
¾ cup water
1 egg yolk
1 tsp olive oil

1. Boil the black cumin seeds in the water for 10 minutes.

2. When the mixture cools down, use a strainer to separate the seeds from the water.

3. Add the raw egg yolk to the black cumin water and mix well to get a creamy solution.

4. Add olive oil to the mixture.

5. Massage it on your scalp and leave for between 30 minutes and 1 hour.

6. Wash off with water. This should be done every week or every other week for best results.

FENNEL

USES

◇ Fennel seeds can help to reduce puffiness under your eyes and also to treat eye infections, such as conjunctivitis.

◇ To get rid of puffy eyes, make a fennel compress for instant relief.

◇ Fennel can also be used as a great toner for skin.

EYE COMPRESS

◇ Mix a little fine fennel seed powder or ground fennel seeds with some water and wrap this mixture in a damp soft cloth.

◇ Use it as a cold compress on red and puffy eyes. This will provide instant relief.

TONER

handful of fennel seeds
1 cup of boiling water
fennel essential oil

1. Add the fennel seeds to boiling water.

2. Leave to cool, and then add a few drops of fennel essential oil to the mixture.

3. Strain the seeds from the liquid.

4. Dab the toner on your face with cotton balls throughout the day. Your skin will feel toned and refreshed.

GARLIC

USES

◊ Garlic benefits the entire body.

◊ It is an amazing aid for reducing spots and acne.

◊ Garlic also stimulates hair growth.

COLD SORE REMEDY

Hold a bit of crushed garlic directly on the cold sore for 2 minutes; its natural anti-inflammatory properties can help reduce pain and swelling.

SPOT REMEDY

Use garlic as a spot treatment on acne and pimples by gently rubbing slices of garlic mixed with honey over them. Remember to do a patch test on your inner wrist first, to make sure you aren't allergic to this remedy.

GARLIC HAIR OIL

Try a garlic-infused hair oil that you can apply every day to your scalp. Simply heat up some coconut oil and simmer some crushed garlic pearls in it, before straining and storing in a bottle.

Caution: Garlic can cause burning sensations if used directly on the skin and in large amounts. Please mix it with other ingredients, such as milk, water or honey before application and only hold it directly on the skin for a short amount of time.

GINGER

USES

◊ Ginger is known to make skin radiant and applying it topically can really make your skin glow.

◊ Ginger is also known to relieve a sore throat.

RADIANCE-BOOSTING GINGER MASK

1 tbsp ginger juice
2 tbsp rosewater
½ tbsp honey

1. Mix all the ingredients together in a small bowl.

2. Apply evenly to the face and then rinse well.

GINGER-LEMON FACE AND BODY SCRUB

¼ cup olive oil
½ cup sugar
2 tsp grated ginger
zest of 1 lemon, plus
    a small squeeze of
    lemon juice

1. Mix all the ingredients together in a small bowl.

2. Apply while in the shower and rinse well.

MASTIC

USES

◊ Mastic oil has a delightful scent and its antiseptic qualities can freshen up your home and kill harmful germs when used as a spray.

◊ It can also be used around the home to repel insects.

◊ Mastic is great for natural dental hygiene.

MASTIC OIL TOOTHPASTE

50ml green tea, cooled
2 drops of mastic oil

1. Mix the ingredients well and use to rinse your mouth after meals or after brushing your teeth. Do not swallow.

2. The fluoride in the green tea, combined with the mastic essential oil's antibacterial action, strengthens the gums, helps prevent tooth decay and leaves your breath fresh.

MINT

USES

◊ Mint has a very soothing and refreshing effect on your skin as it is high in vitamin A, which controls your skin's oil levels and can leave it feeling bright and smooth.

◊ Mint also has strong antibacterial qualities and contains salicylic acid, which can help to prevent and treat acne.

◊ Drinking mint-infused drinks can help to flush toxins from your body.

MINT FACE MASK

handful of crushed
  mint leaves
1 medium-ripe banana
1 tbsp lemon juice

1. Put all the ingredients into a blender and whizz to a smooth paste.

2. Spread over your face and neck and leave for 20 minutes.

3. Rinse with water.

MINT INFUSION DRINK

1 litre filtered water
handful of mint leaves
2 slices of fresh ginger
juice of ½ lemon

1. Pour the water into a jug.

2. Add the mint, ginger and lemon juice.

3. Leave to infuse in the fridge for 7–8 hours.

4. Strain and pour into a glass, add some ice cubes and enjoy!

NUTMEG

USES

◇ Nutmeg has anti-inflammatory properties that can help reduce spots.

◇ It's also known to heal scars caused by sunspots or acne.

◇ Nutmeg can help to clear your pores and reduce the chance of infections, due to its antibacterial elements.

ACNE EXFOLIATING PASTE

50g raw honey
1 tbsp bicarbonate of soda
2 drops clove oil
1 tsp nutmeg
1–2 drops of lemon juice

1. Mix all the ingredients together to make a spreadable paste.

2. Massage into your skin for at least 2 minutes. Your face might feel a bit tingly as the nutmeg gets into your pores, treating the deeper layers of your skin.

3. Rinse well with water.

OREGANO

USES

◊ Oregano has antifungal, antiseptic and antioxidant properties, and benefits the skin by reducing acne or pimples.

◊ Oregano oil is often used in haircare products, as it contains a lot of medicinal and therapeutic properties.

◊ If you have an itchy scalp, oregano oil might be a good option as it has many antibacterial properties.

◊ Oregano oil also fights against dandruff.

FACE TREATMENT

¼ cup aloe vera juice
1 tbsp cucumber juice
3 drops oregano oil

1. Mix all the ingredients together well.

2. Apply the mixture on the affected areas.

3. Leave for 5 minutes, then rinse off with cold water.

HAIR TREATMENT (ITCHY SCALP)

2–3 drops oregano oil
60ml olive oil, coconut
   oil or almond oil

1. Mix 2–3 drops of oregano oil with the other oil.

2. Apply to your scalp, leave for 45 mins and then wash with a medicated shampoo.

ROSEMARY

USES

◊ Rosemary can be used as a great deodorant and air freshener.

DEODORANT

This is a cheap, effective natural deodorant that anyone can make. Just apply apple cider vinegar and rosemary oil to a cotton ball and wipe directly on your underarms.

AIR FRESHENER

This is my favourite natural air freshener. Put a small handful of rosemary, a sliced lemon or orange and a splash of vanilla essence into a pan and simmer very gently all day (watch the water levels). It smells amazing and will freshen the house for days.

ROSEMARY AND AVOCADO HAIR MASK

2 tbsp coconut oil

half a ripe avocado

2 medium eggs

1 tbsp raw honey

5–10 drops rosemary essential oil

5–10 drops lavender essential oil

1. Mix all the ingredients together and apply to your hair.

2. Cover your hair with a shower cap or cling film and leave in for 20 minutes.

3. Wash out throughly and you will be left with silky, shiny hair.

SAFFRON

USES

◊ Massaging with saffron-infused oil can help improve circulation and give skin a beautiful glow.

◊ Saffron can also be used to reduce acne and spots.

INFUSED MASSAGE OIL

3–4 strands of saffron
1 tbsp olive oil

1. Thoroughly mix 3–4 saffron strands with the olive oil.

2. Massage the skin with the oil in upward motions.

3. Wipe the oil off after an hour, using a wet tissue. You can also leave this oil on overnight.

4. Coconut oil, almond oil or sesame oil can also be used instead of olive oil.

5. Repeat every other night.

ACNE AND SPOT TREATMENT

The antibacterial effects of basil and saffron can naturally prevent and cure acne.

4 basil leaves
2 strands of saffron

1. Make a paste by crushing some leaves of basil with a few saffron strands.

2. Dab the paste over the affected areas.

SAGE

USES

◊ Sage is a natural anti-inflammatory that can decrease puffiness and redness caused by ageing and acne. It's often found in anti-ageing serums due to the ferulic acid and vitamin A, which are both antioxidants.

◊ Sage has been used since ancient times to combat hair loss.

◊ Sage infusion has been found to be effective in the treatment of inflamed throat and tonsils as well as ulcerated throat.

TONER

For a great anti-ageing toner, add 1 tsp jobaba and 2 tsp sage oil to a cup of chilled green tea.

HAIR LOSS TREATMENT

Mix 3–4 drops of sage essential oil with equal amounts of rosemary and peppermint essential oils and dilute in 1 tbsp olive oil. Massage your scalp with it twice a day.

SORE THROAT TREATMENT

Boil a pinch of dried sage in about 100ml water and infuse for 15 minutes. Strain and sweeten with honey and use this to gargle twice a day.

THYME

USES

◊ Thyme helps to maintain skin health, by eliminating the bacteria that causes various skin problems.

◊ Thyme oil can enhance oral health.

TONER

Thyme essential oil can be diluted with water and used as a toner to tighten mature skin. It is gentle and can be used on all skin types.

ANTIBACTERIAL MASK

1 medium-ripe banana
3 tbsp chopped thyme
¼ cup yogurt
2 tbsp honey

1. Combine all the ingredients together.

2. Spread the mixture over your clean face, leave for 15 minutes and then rinse with lukewarm water.

MOUTHWASH

You can also use thyme as a mouthwash for maintaining your oral health. Simply add one drop of oil to a cup of warm water. Swish in your mouth and spit it out.

TURMERIC

USES

◇ Turmeric can be used to naturally treat various skin types.

◇ It can help cure stretch marks.

◇ Turmeric can also sooth burns and reduce their scarring.

◇ When applying homemade turmeric masks to your skin, always leave to dry and harden (usually about 30 minutes) before rinsing.

ALL-PURPOSE MASK

1 tsp ground turmeric
1 tsp honey
1 tsp milk or plain yogurt

1. Mix all the ingredients together and apply to face.

2. After 10 minutes, wash off with a warm flannel.

ACNE-PRONE SKIN MASK

1 tsp ground turmeric
1 tbsp chickpea powder
1 tbsp lemon juice
a few drops of water

1. Mix all the ingredients together and apply to face.

2. After 10 minutes, wash off with a warm flannel.

MOISTURISING MASK

¼ tsp ground turmeric
1 egg white
1 tbsp oats

1. Mix all the ingredients together and apply to face.

2. After 10 minutes, wash off with a warm flannel.

BURN CREAM

½ tsp of turmeric

½–1 tsp milk or Greek yogurt to make into a paste

1. Mix a pinch of turmeric and a little milk or yogurt to a thick paste and apply it on the affected area.

2. Let it dry and then wash off gently.

3. Repeat this a few times a day for at least 1–2 weeks, until the burn mark start to fade away.

STRETCH MARK CREAM

½ tsp turmeric

2 strands of saffron

juice of half a lime

1. Mix the ingredients together to make a paste.

2. Apply the paste on the area, leave for 15 minutes and then wash off.

3. Repeat this every day, until the marks fade.

Caution: Turmeric has a tendency to temporarily dye the skin. Although this doesn't happen with everyone who uses it, you may wish to experiment on an inconspicuous part of your body to see how your skin reacts.

If you find turmeric stains your skin, try to remove with a facial toner or make a gentle scrub from sugar and water. If these don't work, moisten a cotton ball in water and rub the stained area; the cotton should draw up the yellow colour. While golden yellow skin will fade with time, getting turmeric on your clothing and other fabrics will leave a mark, so be extra careful.

LIFE HACKS

These are my personal life hacks – shortcuts to get me where I want to go. I am not a doctor so these are not medically proven, but boy, do they work for me!

COLD SHOWERS

OK, so this one is painful and it really doesn't get easier, but it works on SO many levels, and once you start the cold shower ritual, you become strangely addicted. I take cold showers to boost my immune system and since I have been taking them I have not had a cold. They are also fat-burning, as they boost your metabolism and mobilise brown fat. Most people don't know this, but there are two types of fat in your body – brown fat and white fat. White fat is the body fat that we all hate so much. Brown fat is good – it generates heat and keeps your body warm. When you take a cold shower, brown fat is activated, resulting in an increase in energy and calories burned, to keep your body warm. According to studies, cold temperatures can increase brown fat by 15 times the normal amount, which can result in nine pounds of weight loss per year.

Cold showers can also aid your mental well being, as studies have shown that they create a small amount of oxidative stress on your body. While large amounts of oxidative stress are bad, a small amount on a regular basis is good for you. Your nervous system becomes used to the levels, which means it can handle those small amounts. By having a cold shower you make yourself anxious, but this will help you deal with mental anxiety.

FASTING

There is lots of literature out there as to why fasting is good for you but I like to do a regular fast for many reasons. I really believe that it helps my body to re-set. It is one of the most powerful tools on the planet for reversing insulin resistance and stubborn weight loss, and it has long-term protective effects against neurodegenerative diseases such as Alzheimer's and Parkinson's. Reducing insulin in the blood through fasting gives your cells a break, and improves resistance to it. I fast for different lengths of time; I normally do a 24-hour fast from lunchtime on Monday until lunchtime on Tuesday. Then I may do a couple of 16-hour fasts too, but I really try to do a 12 hour fast every day, so I eat supper by 8pm and don't eat again until 8am.

DRINKING

Obviously one must drink in moderation, but to prevent the dreaded hangover, I take a combination of N-acetyl cysteine (NAC), B vitamins, milk thistle and vitamin C before I go out. Then, once I am home, I take a teaspoon of glutathione mixed with water before bed, as it's a powerful anti-oxidant that helps with liver detoxification. This really aids my body and reverses any adverse effects.

TURMERIC SUPPLEMENT

Ok, so I really believe that you should eat your spices, but I understand that life is sometimes too crazy. If that is the case, you should maybe take a turmeric supplement to keep it in your system. There are many good ones, but make sure you take one that is derived from organic turmeric, and has piperine (black pepper) in it. Also, take it with a bit of fat, so taking it at breakfast with your peanut butter on toast would work. I like the ease of an oral spay, which you can also find.

VITAMN D

So many of us are suffer from vitamin D deficiency. It is almost impossible to eat yourself out of this, so I advise that you use a supplement. My favourite, and the one which I found I absorbed best, is the *Better You* spray, which you spray daily into your cheek.

HIGH PHENOLIC EXTRA VIRGIN OLIVE OIL

High phenolic olive oil is beyond organic and beyond extra virgin. While you are using all these delicious spices, I also want to tell you about this amazing olive oil, which will help bring out the nutrients in them. I am now taking Atsas oil as a nutrient and make sure I always have a raw tablespoon of it on one of the things I am eating every day. It is additional insurance to help anti-ageing and weight balance.

Over two thousand years ago, Hippocrates and Dioscorides referred to early harvest olive oil as 'medicinal'. Modern science has identified the polyphenols, or more accurately, the phenolic compounds, that are health-protective and we continue to research the effectiveness of them for the prevention and treatment of many of today's chronic illnesses, including heart attack and stroke, high blood pressure, rheumatoid arthritis, obesity, Alzheimer's, Parkinson's, Type 2 diabetes and cancer.

The reason I am telling you about this amazing olive oil is that the information about it has only just been quantified. In 2012, the EU passed regulation 432/2012 regarding labelling. This regulation stated that olive oils with over 250 mg/kg polyphenols can put a health claim on the label as it reduces LDL oxidation. In the same year, Dr Prokopios Magiatis and Dr Eleni Melliou of the University of Athens discovered a method to accurately measure individual phenolic compounds in olive oil using Nuclear Magnetic Resonance (NMR) The following year, they invented a test kit to measure the combined phenolic compounds Oleocanthal and Oleacein.

It is well-known that most illness is the result of inflammation, and the phenolic compound Oleocanthal is known for its anti-inflammatory properties. Oleacein is a known antioxidant and these compounds are only found in extra virgin olive oil. EVOOs that test well in these and other phenols are allowed to place the EU regulation 432/2012 on the label in the EU and, since olive oil is a natural food, daily consumption of High Phenolic EVOO is a smart choice for optimum health, vitality and longevity.

To find out more and to buy High Phenolic Extra Virgin Olive Oil go to: www.aristoleo.com. My favourite is from www.atsas.com and www.strakka-organics.myshopify.com

THE
RECIPES

RECIPES FOR

AGEING WELL

CORIANDER, ROSEMARY,
BASIL, MASTIC

ROASTED OCTOPUS
WITH LEMON AND PARSLEY

This is the most simple and delicious octopus recipe you will ever find.

SERVES 4 AS PART OF A MEZE

1 whole octopus,
cleaned and prepared
(ask your fishmonger
to do this for you)

extra virgin olive oil

4 large rosemary sprigs

juice of 2 lemons

a handful of flat-leaf
parsley, chopped

To serve

tomato and onion
or Greek salad

lemon wedges

crusty bread

Preheat the oven to 150°C/300°F/Gas Mark 2.

Lay the prepared octopus in a large, shallow roasting dish, drizzle generously with olive oil and add the rosemary sprigs. Cover completely with foil.

Roast in the oven for 1½–2 hours, depending on size, until very tender.

When cooked, transfer the octopus to a plate and, using scissors, cut into bite-sized pieces.

Whisk a little olive oil and lemon juice together (a 2:1 ratio of oil to juice) to make an emulsion. Stir in the chopped parsley, and drizzle over the warm octopus.

Serve with tomato and onion or Greek salad, and lemon wedges. Mop up the juices with crusty bread.

GRIDDLED HERRING
AND NUTMEG MASH

This recipe also works well with mackerel and is bursting with omega 3.

SERVES 2

2 herrings, filleted

2 tbsp olive oil

juice of ½ lemon

1 tsp ground coriander

2 garlic cloves, crushed

salt and freshly ground
black pepper

1 small bunch of coriander

For the mash

500g potatoes,
skin on, cubed

30g butter

½ tsp ground turmeric

½ tsp ground nutmeg

full-fat milk

For the veg

2 large fresh beetroot,
skin on, scrubbed

8 asparagus stems

olive oil, for drizzling

For the dressing

2 tbsp Greek yogurt

1 tbsp horseradish sauce

1 tbsp coriander
leaves, chopped

½ tsp ground coriander
seeds

½ tsp fennel seeds

Put the herrings in a bowl with the oil, lemon juice, ground coriander, garlic, salt and pepper. Mix well, cover, and allow to marinate in the fridge for at least 20 minutes.

Put the cubed potatoes in a saucepan of salted boiling water and cook until soft. Drain and set aside.

Melt the butter in a pan and add the turmeric. Put the nutmeg, salt and pepper in a bowl with the potatoes. Add the butter and turmeric mix and mash, adding enough milk to loosen. Transfer the mash to a warm dish and put in a low (150°C/300°F/Gas Mark 2) oven to stay warm.

For the veg, slice the beetroot into 6 rings and snap off the hard ends of the asparagus. Drizzle both with oil and season with salt and pepper.

Heat a stovetop griddle pan until hot. Add the beetroot and asparagus and griddle for 10 minutes on each side until chargrilled and cooked through. Set aside.

Pat the skin of the fish dry, then score it. Cook the herring fillets on the griddle pan, skin-side down, for 3–4 minutes. When golden brown and crisp, squeeze the lemon over the fish, then turn over and cook for a further 2 minutes.

For the dressing, mix the Greek yogurt, horseradish, coriander leaves, coriander and fennel seeds in a bowl.

To serve, place a large dollop of the mash on each plate, and add the asparagus and beetroot, followed by the herring. Spoon over the Greek yogurt dressing, and garnish with coriander.

COURGETTE, FETA AND CHILLI SAVOURY MUFFINS

These are delicious warm or cold. I like to serve them as a savoury breakfast muffin or as an accompaniment to soup.

MAKES 8–10

75ml olive oil

1 onion, chopped

2 medium eggs

1 tsp oregano, chopped

1 tsp basil, chopped

150g feta cheese, crumbled

1–2 red chillies, finely chopped (optional, but give a great kick)

1 large courgette, finely grated

1 small tin (140g) sweetcorn, drained (optional)

150g wholemeal spelt flour

1½ tsp baking powder

100ml milk

salt and freshly ground black pepper

Preheat the oven to 180°C/350°F/Gas Mark 4. Lightly grease 8–10 muffin cases with olive oil and put in a muffin tin.

Heat 2 tbsp of olive oil in a frying pan over a low heat, add the onion and fry for 5 minutes, or until softened.

Beat the eggs in a bowl, then add the remaining olive oil, the oregano, basil, feta, chilli (if using) courgette and sweetcorn. Add the flour and baking powder and enough milk to make a batter mixture.

Place 2 heaped tbsp of the batter into each muffin case and bake in the oven for around 25–30 minutes until they are golden and firm to the touch. Add salt and pepper to taste.

SPICY LAMB CHOPS
WITH GREEK-STYLE MINT SAUCE

This recipe is from my daughter Antigoni, and it's a real family favourite. We all become cavemen when eating these chops – we literally lick the last of the tangy mint sauce off the bones.

SERVES 4

For the chops

10 tsp salt

5 tsp freshly ground
    black pepper

2½ tsp ground coriander

1¼ tsp cayenne pepper

10 garlic cloves, crushed

5 splashes of
    Worcestershire sauce

juice of 2 lemons

zest of 5 lemons

16 lamb chops or cutlets

olive oil, for drizzling

rosemary sprigs

For the mint sauce

4 bunches of mint

30g of flat leaf parsley

8 anchovy fillets

4 garlic cloves

chilli flakes, to taste

olive oil, as needed

lemon juice, as needed

a pinch of salt (optional)

For the lamb chops, stir the salt, black pepper, ground coriander, cayenne, crushed garlic, Worcestershire sauce and lemon juice and zest together in a bowl large enough to hold all the chops or cutlets.

Season the lamb on both sides with the spice rub, then allow to stand at room temperature while you make the mint sauce. (You can also do this step the night before or in the morning and keep in the fridge until you make the sauce.)

For the mint sauce, place the mint, parsley, anchovies, garlic and chilli flakes in a food processor and whizz, adding olive oil and lemon juice as you go, until the sauce is loose enough to drizzle. Taste and add salt if needed, though the anchovies should give it enough salt.

Turn the grill to a medium-high heat.

Drizzle some oil over the lamb chops and place rosemary sprigs on the top. For extra flavour, stick half a garlic clove in the fat of each of the chops.

Grill the lamb until cooked to your liking, about 2–3 minutes on each side for medium rare. Serve with jewelled couscous or baked sweet potato and green beans.

PATATES SPASTES
(SMASHED NEW POTATOES
WITH CORIANDER SEEDS)

These little chaps neither sound nor look very endearing, but they taste delicous. They are so addictive – once you've eaten one you can't stop until they've all gone! I wonder whether 'smashed' refers to the state of the potato after being bashed open or the effect of them being steeped in wine . . . A bit of both?

SERVES 4

organic rapeseed oil, for deep-frying

500g small whole new potatoes, washed and patted dry

150ml red wine

1 heaped tbsp coriander seeds, hand ground in mortar and pestle

a pinch of salt

Pour enough rapeseed oil into a deep heavy-based pan to fill it to one third. Heat the oil until it is shimmering, then fry the whole potatoes, a few at a time, for 10 minutes, or until golden brown and soft inside.

Transfer the cooked potatoes to kitchen paper to drain, while you cook the remaining batches.

Drain the remaining oil, put the potatoes back into the hot pan, and dry-fry over a medium-to- high heat, bashing them lightly with a wooden spoon or a potato masher so they crack open, but do not split.

After a few minutes, add the wine, coriander seeds and salt and simmer for 5–10 minutes, shaking the pan occasionally.

Serve immediately.

LAVENDER AND BLUEBERRY TEA BREAD

To make lavender sugar, add fresh lavender (if it's available) to light muscovado or demerara sugar in a jar, cover with a lid and leave for at least three days before using. If you don't have any fresh lavender, add a drop of lavender extract to the sugar.

SERVES 8–10

125g unsalted butter
at room temperature,
plus 1 tbsp butter,
for greasing

100g lavender sugar
(see intro)

2 medium eggs, beaten

400g fresh blueberries

250g wholemeal
self-raising flour

1 tsp baking powder

1 tsp ground cinnamon

1 tsp ground mastic
or ½ tsp cloves

For the icing (optional)

250g instant royal icing

violet food colouring

8 lavender sprigs

Preheat the oven to 180°C/350°F/Gas Mark 4. Grease the base and line a 900g loaf tin.

Cream the butter and sugar together until pale and fluffy. Beat in the eggs a little at a time. Add the blueberries and mix well.

Sift all the dry ingredients together, and add to the wet ingredients, folding in until combined. Transfer the batter to the prepared tin.

Bake in the oven for 50–60 minutes until risen and firm to the touch. Allow to cool on a wire rack.

Once the cake has cooled, make the icing. Mix the instant royal icing according to the packet instructions and add the food colouring, a little at a time, to get the right shade. Drizzle over the cooled cake, then decorate the cake with lavender and allow to set.

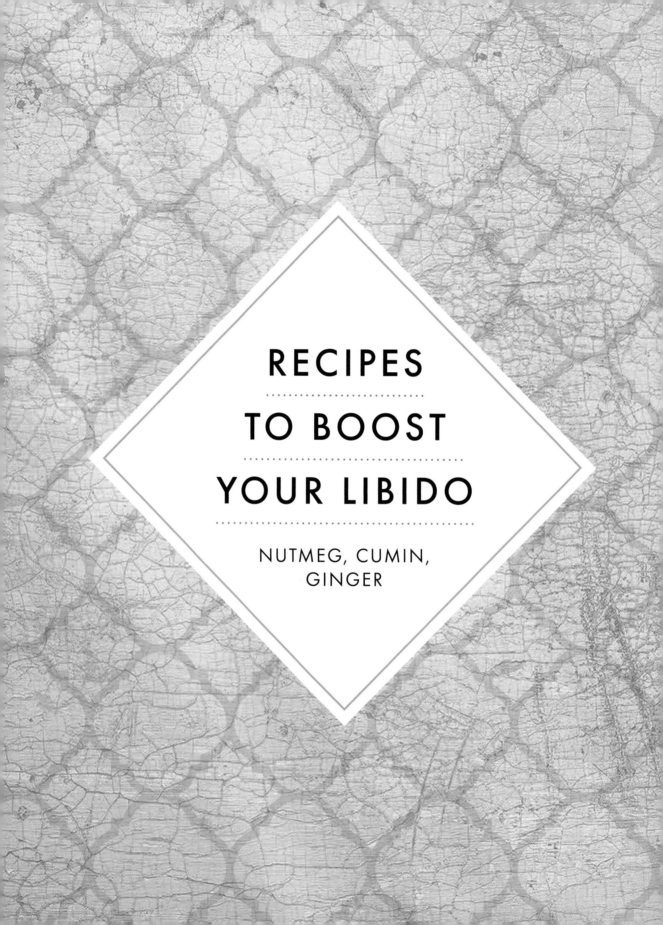

RECIPES
TO BOOST
YOUR LIBIDO

NUTMEG, CUMIN,
GINGER

MOROCCAN TOMATO AND PEPPER SALAD

A traditional tomato salad that is perfect for late summer when there's a glut of tomatoes.

SERVES 2

4 green peppers

4 fresh tomatoes

2 tbsp olive oil

½ tsp freshly ground black pepper

1 tsp ground cumin

1 tsp paprika

4 garlic cloves, finely chopped

8 mint leaves, finely chopped

a pinch of salt

a squeeze of lemon juice

a small bunch of parsley, finely chopped

Grill the green peppers over a flame until the skins are blackened and blistered all over, then put in an airtight or ziplock plastic bag for 15 minutes. Peel off the skin and remove the seeds, then cut into fine strips. Peel and dice the tomatoes.

Place the oil, diced tomatoes, spices and garlic in a pan and cook over a medium heat for 10 minutes. As you cook, mash the tomatoes into a paste, then add the green pepper strips and mint and cook for a further 5 minutes. Season with salt, add a squeeze of lemon juice and sprinkle parsley over the top.

CHICKPEA-FILLED FILO TRIANGLES

This is one of the dishes that's on my vegan menu for The Real Greek. It has proved to be a very popular as it has the perfect balance of aroma and spice. If you fancy trying them but don't want to cook them yourself, you could always pop in to The Real Greek and give them a go!

MAKES 12–16

1 pack filo pastry

olive oil, for brushing

For the filling

2 x 400g tinned chickpeas, drained

1 onion, cut into quarters

1 tsp ground cumin

½ tsp ground turmeric

40g sundried tomatoes

1 small red chilli, very finely chopped

3 garlic cloves, crushed

zest and juice of 1 lemon

2 tbsp olive oil

30g flat leaf parsley, finely chopped

salt and freshly ground black pepper

black and white sesame seeds for sprinkling (optional)

Preheat the oven to 180°C/350°F/Gas Mark 4 and line a baking tray with baking paper.

Place all the filling ingredients except from the seasame seeds into a food processor and blitz into a coarse paste.

Remove the filo pastry from the wrapper and unroll onto a clean work surface. Cut through the centre vertically so you have two even sections. Place one on top of the other. Use two sheets per triangle.

Place 1 heaped tsp (do not overfill) of filling at the bottom of each strip and then start folding the pastry around the filling. Seal the triangle with a dab of olive oil.

Lightly brush with olive oil (you don't want the pastry to be oily) and sprinkle with a little salt.

Place the pastries on the lined baking tray, under damp kitchen paper, and continue until you have used up all the filling or pastry sheets. Sprinkle them with dark and light sesame seeds (if using) Bake for 12–15 minutes until golden.

GREEN SHAKSHUKA EGGS

Use whatever veg you have in your cupboards to make these super-tasty,
pimped-up breakfast eggs.

SERVES 4

240g baby spinach

1 bunch of spring
  onions, sliced

2 green peppers,
  deseeded and sliced

3 garlic cloves, crushed

1 tbsp organic rapeseed
  oil or organic hemp oil

½ green chilli, deseeded
  and diced

½ tsp ground cumin

½ tsp smoked paprika

½ tsp ground coriander

salt and freshly ground
  black pepper

4 medium eggs

50g frozen peas,
  defrosted

100g feta, crumbled

2 tbsp fresh dill

toasted sourdough,
  to serve

Wilt the spinach in a large shallow pan over a medium heat with a splash of water. Remove from the pan and squeeze out all the liquid. Set aside.

In the same pan, gently sweat the spring onions, peppers and garlic in the oil for a few minutes. Stir through the chilli, cumin, smoked paprika and coriander, and then add the spinach. Season with salt and pepper and mix well.

Make 4 wells in the spinach mixture and crack the eggs into them.

Scatter the peas in evenly, cover with a lid and cook for 8–10 minutes, until the egg whites are set.

Sprinkle over the feta and dill, and serve with sourdough toast.

WHOLEMEAL PIZZA BASE

I like to add some spices to the base, such as aniseed or ground cumin. If you are adding these, then put them in with the flour.

SERVES 6

1 tbsp caster sugar

300ml lukewarm water

2½ tsp fast-action dried yeast

3 tbsp olive oil, plus extra for coating

1 tsp fine sea salt

375g strong wholemeal bread flour

½ tsp ground cumin

Pizza sauces and Toppings (see page 205)

Place the sugar and lukewarm water in a large bowl and stir. Sprinkle the yeast on top and leave for 5–10 minutes until it is foamy. Add the olive oil and salt, then the flour and cumin and mix together to form a dough.

Take the dough from the bowl and knead on a lightly floured work surface for 10 minutes.

Coat the bowl with a little olive oil and place the kneaded dough back in the bowl. Cover with a damp tea towel and allow to rise in a warm room for around 1–1½ hours, until it has doubled in size.

Once the dough has increased in size, place a pizza stone (if you have one, otherwise use an upturned flat baking tray) in the oven, and preheat to 240°C/450°F/Gas Mark 8.

Punch the dough down and tip it out of the bowl. Divide it into 4 balls, then stretch out each portion of dough with your hands or roll with a rolling pin. Put the pizza sauce and whichever toppings you like on top of the dough. Use a pizza paddle or cake server to place your pizza on the pizza stone or baking tray, closing the oven door quickly to retain the heat. Bake in the oven for 12–15 minutes until the pizza is cooked.

PIZZA SAUCE AND TOPPINGS

MAKES 4 PIZZAS

500ml tomato passata

3 garlic cloves, crushed

3 tbsp tomato pureé

1 tsp salt

1 tsp freshly ground black pepper

1 tsp ground cumin

1 tsp balsamic vinegar

½ tsp caster sugar

½ tsp dried chilli flakes (optional)

To make the sauce, put all the ingredients in a saucepan and cook for 10–15 minutes until thickened. Taste and adjust the seasoning if necessary.

PIZZA TOPPING SUGGESTIONS

CHEESE
◇ Mozzarella
◇ Burrata
◇ Cheddar
◇ Mascarpone

MEAT AND FISH
◇ Pepperoni
◇ Ham
◇ Chorizo
◇ Ham
◇ Parma ham/Prosciutto
◇ Chicken
◇ Anchovies

VEGETABLES
◇ Mushrooms
◇ Sweetcorn
◇ Pineapple
◇ Olives
◇ Onions
◇ Peppers

SALAD
◇ Spinach
◇ Rocket

PESTO
◇ Basil
◇ Oregano
◇ Thyme

MY HOT SPICE PASTE

This is my family's ketchup – it can be used as an accompaniment or as the versatile base for most sauces

MAKES 1 JAR

2 roasted red peppers
    from a jar
5 garlic cloves
400g tin chopped
    tomatoes, drained
    (include the juice for a
    more saucy consistency)
1 tbsp smoked paprika
1–2 red chillies
1 red bird's eye chilli
5–6 tbsp olive oil
salt and freshly ground
    black pepper

For the spice mix

1 tsp cumin seeds
1 tsp fennel seeds
2 tsp coriander seeds
1 tsp dried chilli flakes

For the spice mix, toast all the spices in a pan over a medium heat until fragrant. Grind in a mortar and pestle until fine and set aside.

In a blender or food processor, combine all the remaining ingredients together with the spices and blend until you have a vibrant red paste. Season to taste. If you like the paste hotter, add the extra red chilli. Transfer to clean jars, cover with lids and store in the fridge for up to 1 month.

RHUBARB AND CUSTARD MESSY BAKE

This recipe does exactly what it says on the tin – it's messy but completely delicious.

SERVES 6

400g rhubarb,
   trimmed and cut
   into 4cm lengths

2 pieces of stem ginger in
   syrup, finely chopped

2–3 tbsp fresh
   orange juice

100g golden caster sugar,
   plus 1–2 tbsp extra for
   sprinkling

150g wholemeal flour

1 tsp baking powder

½ tsp vanilla powder

¼ tsp ground nutmeg

¼ tsp ground cloves

a pinch of salt

45g unsalted butter, diced

4 tbsp whole milk

500ml tub fresh vanilla
   custard

Preheat the oven to 190°C/375°F/Gas Mark 5.

Place the rhubarb, ginger, orange juice and 50g of the sugar in an ovenproof dish and bake in the oven for 25 minutes, or until softened.

Stir the flour, baking powder, vanilla powder, nutmeg, cloves, remaining sugar and salt together in a bowl. Add the butter and rub it in, then stir in the milk and bring together with your hands.

Take small spoonfuls of the dough and place on top of the rhubarb. Scatter over the extra 1–2 tbsp sugar and bake for 30–35 minutes, until the topping is golden and cooked all the way through.

Serve with custard.

RECIPES

FOR A BETTER

MOOD

SAFFRON, CACAO,
BLACK PEPPER

AROMATIC CHICKEN CURRY

As with all curries, this is the perfect dish to make the day before and eat the next day.

SERVES 4

8 chicken thighs

2 onions, sliced

500g Charlotte
    potatoes, halved

olive oil, for cooking

2 tsp fennel seeds

2 tsp black mustard seeds

2 tsp ground coriander

1 tsp ground turmeric

salt and freshly ground
    black pepper

2x 400ml tinned light
    coconut milk

10 curry leaves

200g frozen peas

150g green beans,
    trimmed

2 tbsp coriander leaves

For the marinade

8 tbsp sunflower oil

4 tsp grated ginger

4 garlic cloves, crushed

zest and juice of 3 limes

2 tsp ground turmeric

4 tsp ground coriander

2 tsp garam masala

To serve

mango chutney

lime wedges

Mix all the marinade ingredients together in a bowl large enough to hold the chicken thighs. Add the chicken and turn until they are coated. Cover with cling film or a plate, and allow to marinate in the fridge for at least 30 minutes, but preferably overnight.

Preheat the oven to 200°C/400°C/Gas Mark 6.

Arrange the sliced onions in a single layer on the base of a deep roasting tin, and put the chicken pieces on top. Tip the potatoes into the bowl that the chicken was marinating in and toss until coated. Add them to the tin around the chicken and roast for 45 minutes, until everything is golden and crisp. Keep checking on the thighs and potatoes while they are roasting and turn them over if they are getting too cooked. Add a tiny bit of oil to prevent them from sticking, if necessary.

Whisk the fennel, mustard seeds, coriander, turmeric and 1 tsp salt and pepper into the coconut milk in a bowl. Add the curry leaves and then pour over the chicken. Return to the oven for another 30 minutes. Stir in the peas and green beans and bake for a further 10 minutes, adding a little water if there's not enough to coat the peas and beans.

Sprinkle with coriander and serve with mango chutney and lime wedges.

BAKED FETA SAGANAKI

Feta is such a wonderful cheese. If you can, try to get the organic oak-aged one as it tastes wonderful. This is the simplest of all my recipes – it's so quick and easy to make it. You can make it either in a large rustic sharing dish or in individual portions.

SERVES 4

200g feta

2 peppers of any colour

1 tbsp Kalamata olives

200g cherry tomatoes, halved

1 green chilli, thinly sliced

1 tsp oregano

2 tbsp olive oil

zest and juice of 1 lemon

sumac, for sprinkling

freshly ground
    black pepper

Preheat the oven to 180°C/350°F/Gas Mark 4.

If making individual portions, divide the feta into 4 portions and place on a large square of foil or baking paper. Add the peppers, olives, cherry tomatoes, chilli and oregano, then drizzle in the olive oil. Toss the ingredients until they are coated in the oil, then make a little sealed pouch and place in the oven.

If you are making it to share, grease a baking tray or ovenproof dish, then toss all the ingredients as above and give them a good mix.

Bake in the oven for 15–20 minutes. Serve immediately with lemon zest and juice, sumac and black pepper sprinkled over the top.

VENISON STEW

This is a real family favourite – it is a wonderful, warming stew that's brimming with health-giving spices. It freezes well too, so when I know I'm going to have a busy time or be away I make up big batches and pop them in the freezer.

SERVES 8

1 tbsp olive oil

25g butter

2 onions, finely diced

4 rashers streaky bacon, chopped

500g mixed mushrooms, sliced

6 garlic cloves, 4 finely chopped, 2 crushed

2kg venison, diced

½ bottle red wine

300ml strong beef stock

3 tbsp redcurrant jelly

250g Chantenay carrots, peeled and kept whole

2 parsnips, cut into large slices

1 tbsp ground turmeric

1 tsp freshly ground black pepper

3 rosemary sprigs

6 sage leaves, finely chopped

2 small hot red chillies

50g cornflour

To serve

wilted spinach

mashed potatoes

Preheat the oven to 150°C/300°F/Gas Mark 2 (or use aslow cooker if you have one).

Heat the oil and butter in a lidded casserole dish on the hob. Add the onions and cook until soft and golden.

Add the bacon and mushrooms and cook for a further 2 minutes, then add the garlic and cook for another minute.

Brown the venison in a frying pan in batches, so as not to overcrowd the pan, adding it to the casserole as you do.

Add the wine, stock, jelly, carrots, parsnips, turmeric, black pepper, rosemary, sage and chillies and bring to the boil.

Either transfer the stew to the slow cooker and cook on low for up to 7 hours, or place it in the oven with the lid on and cook for 2 hours.

Half an hour before the end of cooking, mix the cornflour with a little water to make a paste and stir it into the casserole. Cover and return to the oven for a further 30 minutes.

Serve with wilted spinach and mashed potatoes.

SPINACH, LEEK AND MUSHROOM PIE

This is my version of the classic Greek dish, spanakopita.

SERVES 4–6

1 pack filo pastry
(250–270g)

olive oil, for brushing

sesame seeds,
for sprinkling

For the filling

450g fresh spinach

450g leeks, sliced

4 garlic cloves, crushed

2 tbsp olive oil

200g mushrooms,
chopped

½ tsp grated nutmeg

300g feta, crumbled

15 mint leaves,
finely chopped

1 tsp freshly ground
black pepper

zest of 1 lemon, plus
squeeze of juice

Preheat the oven to 180°C/350°F/Gas Mark 4. Grease a 23cm deep loose-bottomed flan tin.

For the filling, wash the spinach leaves and add to a pan with only the water that clings to them. Cover and cook gently until tender. Allow to cool slightly, then squeeze out the excess water and chop.

Soften the leeks and garlic in the oil over a medium heat. Add the mushrooms and fry for a further 2 minutes. Remove from the heat and add the chopped spinach, nutmeg, feta and mint. Season with black pepper and lemon juice and zest and mix very well.

Line the prepared flan tin with one-third of the filo sheets, brushing each sheet with olive oil and leaving an overhang to fold over the filling.

Spread half of the filling into the lined flan case and press down evenly. Cover with half of the remaining filo sheets, again brushing each sheet with olive oil. Spread the rest of the filling on top and fold the overhanging pastry over the top.

Finely shred the remaining filo sheets and scrunch them over the top, to enclose the filling completely.

Brush with olive oil and sprinkle with sesame seeds, then bake in the oven for 30–35 minutes until golden brown.

Carefully remove from the tin, cut into wedges and serve.

SLOW-COOKED PORK
AND FIERY MINTY SALSA

I like to put the pulled pork in a brioche bun and eat it as a slider, or make up a lettuce batch ready to serve as a canapé. Or in the cold winter months I like to serve this with my Nutmeg Mash (see page 192) and steamed veg, such as broccoli, kale or peas.

SERVES 6–8

1kg boned out pork shoulder or leg, cut into large chunks, fat left on

salt and freshly ground black pepper

2 tbsp organic cold-pressed rapeseed oil

1 bulb of garlic, halved horizontally

100ml apple cider vinegar

400ml fresh chicken stock

1 star anise

2 large cinnamon sticks

6 cloves

3 rosemary sprigs

zest and juice of 1 orange

flatbread or gem lettuce leaves, to serve

For the salsa

2 chillies, deseeded and halved

1 orange, peeled and cut into segments

1 apple, peeled, cored and cut into wedges

½ garlic clove

8 mint leaves

1 tbsp lemon juice

Preheat the oven to 190°C/375°F/Gas Mark 5.

Season the meat with salt and pepper. Heat a frying pan until hot, then add half the oil and half the pork. Leave the pork until it can move without sticking, then turn over and seal on all sides. Once the pork is sealed and browned, transfer it to a heavy-based ovenproof saucepan and repeat the process.

Brown the cut side of the garlic in the pork fat and add to the saucepan, followed by all the other ingredients.

Bring the liquid to the boil, then cover the pan with a lid and put into the oven. Reduce the oven temperature to 160°C/325°F/Gas Mark 3 and cook, covered, for 3 hours. Check after 2 ½ hours that the liquid hasn't evaporated.

Once cooked, allow to cool a little, then shred the meat with two forks and return to the sauce.

Meanwhile, make the salsa. Place the chillies in a blender with the orange segments, apple wedges, garlic and mint and process until nearly smooth. While the motor is running, slowly add the lemon juice. Season to taste and serve immediately. If you prefer a chunkier salsa, cut everything into small pieces and don't blend.

To serve, place some of the pulled pork either on a warmed flatbread or a piece of gem lettuce, then add a teaspoon of the salsa on top.

BABY CUTTLEFISH

You can find baby cuttlefish in Chinese, Thai or Vietnamese supermarkets, but if
you are struggling to find them, replace with baby octopus.

SERVES 4 AS A MAIN COURSE

100ml soy sauce

a dash of oyster sauce

50ml olive oil

1 tbsp brown sugar

1 large chilli, finely
  chopped

1 tbsp grated ginger

a pinch of saffron strands

1 heaped tbsp toasted
  sesame seeds

zest of ½ orange

juice of 1 orange

salt and freshly ground
  black pepper

100ml soy sauce

a dash of oyster sauce

50ml olive oil

1 tbsp brown sugar

1 large chilli, finely
  chopped

1 tbsp grated ginger

a pinch of saffron strands

1 heaped tbsp toasted
  sesame seeds

zest of ½ orange

juice of 1 orange

1kg baby cuttlefish,
  kept whole and spine
  removed

Put all the ingredients, except the cuttlefish, into a large bowl.
Taste the marinade and adjust if it needs more honey or chillies.
Add the cuttlefish to the marinade, cover, and leave in the
fridge for at least 2 hours, or overnight if possible.

Barbecue for 2–3 minutes on each side, being careful not to
overcook, and serve immediately. You could also cook the fish
on a griddle pan or under the grill, if you prefer.

TAHINI AND CHOCOLATE BAKE

Tahini is such a wonderful addition to cakes – it adds moisture and depth to the flavour.
These are like Middle Eastern brownies.

MAKES 16

250g unsalted butter,
 plus extra for greasing

250g good-quality
 dark chocolate (at
 least 70% cocoa
 solids), roughly
 chopped

4 medium eggs

280g caster sugar

30g cocoa powder

120g wholemeal flour

½ tsp salt

200g halva, broken
 into 2cm pieces

35g tahini

Preheat the oven to 200°C/400°F/Gas Mark 6. Grease and line a baking tin with baking paper and set aside.

Gently melt the butter and chocolate together in a pan, then set aside until it has cooled to room temperature.

Whisk the eggs and sugar in a bowl. Add the melted chocolate mixture and fold through gently.

Sift the cocoa, flour and salt into another bowl and then gently fold it into the chocolate mixture. Gently fold in the halva pieces and then spoon the mixture into the prepared baking tin.

Dollop a small teaspoon of tahini into the mix in about 10 different places, then use a skewer to swirl through, creating a marble effect.

Bake in the oven for 20–25 minutes until the middle has a slight wobble and is gooey inside. Don't worry if it seems a little undercooked as it will firm up as it cools. Once cool, cut into squares and serve.

RECIPES TO

·····················

BALANCE YOUR

·····················

HORMONES

·····················

SAGE, TURMERIC,
CHILLI

MEATBALLS THREE WAYS

If you have a fussy eater in your family as I do, this is an amazing way to get vegetables into their diet. This recipe also works well if you want to make canapés – they are wonderful if you want to serve them like a kofta, perfect with my fresh tomato sauce and completely heavenly when put into a ciabatta bun and made into a sub! You will need a food processor for this recipe.

SERVES 6 AS A MEAL OR 12 AS CANAPÉS

For the tomato sauce

3–4 tbsp olive oil

10 large tomatoes, roughly chopped

5 cloves garlic

salt and freshly ground pepper

handful of fresh basil leaves

2 tsp of dried oregano

balsamic vinegar

500ml tomato passata

For the meatballs

4 cloves garlic

2 onions

1 or 2 fresh chillies

1 bunch parsley

2 sweet potatoes, chopped

2 carrots, chopped

3 preserved lemons, chopped, pips removed

2 slices of wholemeal bread

small bunch of mint

1 tsp turmeric

1 tsp of black pepper

3 tsp sumac

500g organic minced pork, lamb or chicken

2 medium eggs

40ml olive oil

Preheat the oven at 180°C/350°F/Gas Mark 4.

First make the tomato sauce. Add the oil to a large saucepan. Add the garlic and tomatoes and simmer until soft. Then, with a potato masher, mash it all down. Add all the other ingredients and simmer for 20–30 minutes.

Next, make the meatballs. Put everything apart from the spices, meat and eggs into the food processor in batches and blend to a coarse paste.

Place the spices, meat and eggs in a large bowl. The only way to mix this is to get your hands in and really mix everything together.

Line two baking trays with baking paper and start to form the meatballs, making them golf-ball size. Lay them on the tray and then put in the oven at for 30 minutes, turning over once halfway through. These are now ready to serve one of three ways:

As a canapé: Add sticks and serve, or you could also put them on a gem lettuce leaf and drizzle with tahini for extra zing.

Pasta: You could add the meatballs and tomato sauce to a dish of pasta for the perfect main course.

Meatball sub: Lightly toast some buns, add 2–3 meatballs per bun and plenty of tomato sauce, scatter mozzarella on top and toast under a medium-to-hot grill, until the cheese has melted.

BLUE CHEESE AND FIG TART

This tart is such a lovely showstopper. I make it when I'm hosting a drinks party because it's as delicous as it is beautiful.

SERVES 6–8

50g butter

4 tbsp olive oil

5 large red
onions, sliced

1 tbsp brown sugar

200g baby courgettes,
cut diagonally

1 red pepper, sliced

1 yellow pepper, sliced

1 aubergine, sliced

2 tsp sumac

½ tsp ground turmeric

1 tsp freshly ground black
pepper

a pinch of salt

3 garlic cloves, sliced

1 pack ready rolled
puff pastry

8 figs, quartered

a drizzle of pomegranate
molasses

2 black garlic cloves,
finely sliced

250g blue cheese,
crumbled

bunch of basil leaves

Preheat the oven to 190°C/375°F/Gas Mark 5.

Place half the butter and half the oil with the onions and sugar in a heavy-based pan and caramelise on a medium heat until the onions have darkened. Remove from the pan and set aside.

Add the remaining butter and oil to the pan, then add the courgettes, pepper and aubergine and sauté for 5–8 minutes until softened. Add the sumac, turmeric, pepper, salt and garlic and cook for about 10 minutes, until just starting to colour.

Line a large baking tray with baking paper. Roll out the puff pastry until it is over the edges and then fold it back in to make a border.

Evenly distribute the caramelised onions inside the border of the puff pastry, then do the same with the vegetable mixture. Scatter over the figs and bake in the oven for 20 minutes.

Drizzle with the pomegranate molasses and scatter over the black garlic, blue cheese and basil. Serve immediately, being careful not to burn your mouth on the hot figs!

KEFTHEDES VEG-AND-SPICE-STYLE

For this recipe I use my food processor and blitz everything, as I want my fussy son to eat veg!
These meatballs can be eaten in a bun like a burger but I always serve them with a large salad
and lots of houmous. You can also eat them cold, and they make great canapés. Serve them
small and round on a stick, like lollipops (the cooking time then would be 20–25 minutes) and
drizzle with tahini and pomegranate molasses.

SERVES 6–8

1 large onion, blitzed

4 garlic cloves, blitzed

2 small sweet potatoes,
  grated then blitzed

1 bunch of parsley, blitzed

2 carrots, grated

500g minced pork or beef
  or lamb or turkey

1 heaped tsp ground
  cinnamon

1 tsp salt

1 tsp freshly ground
  black pepper

1 tbsp sumac

1 tsp ground turmeric

1–2 red or green chillies,
  blitzed (optional)

2 medium eggs

Preheat the oven to 180°C/350°F/Gas Mark 4. Line a
baking tray with baking paper.

Place all the ingredients, except the eggs, in a large bowl
and then add the eggs. Using your hands, mix everything
together for 3–5 minutes. Form the mixture into large
meatballs, or burgers.

Arrange the meatballs on the prepared baking tray and
bake in the oven for 30–35 minutes. Check that they are
cooked through before serving.

HOUMOUS SO MANY WAYS!

This is the most basic houmous recipe, but I've also added some variations that I love.
I'm very lazy so I make it all in the food processor.

MAKES ENOUGH FOR 6–8 PEOPLE

*400g can chickpeas,
   drained and water
   reserved*

3 tbsp tahini

juice of 2–3 lemons

5 garlic cloves, crushed

½ tsp ground turmeric

*½ tsp freshly ground
   black pepper*

a pinch of salt

To garnish

olive oil

chopped parsley

a pinch of paprika

Drain the chickpeas, reserving some of the brine, and rinse under cold running water. Transfer to a large bowl.

Process the chickpeas in a food processor or hand blender for a fine texture. Alternatively, mash by hand for a coarser dip.

In a separate bowl, mix the tahini, lemon juice, chickpea water and garlic together to a runny consistency. Mix into the chickpeas with the turmeric and pepper, then season with salt to taste. Adjust the consistency and taste to suit with either extra lemon juice or chickpea brine.

Chill for several hours to allow the flavours to infuse. Serve garnished with a drizzle of olive oil and a sprinkling of chopped parsley and a pinch of paprika.

OR just put everything in to the food processor, starting with the garlic, then adding the chickpeas, liquid and remaining ingredients. This is such a simple way of making fresh houmous and it tastes amazing.

CHILLI AND CUMIN HOUMOUS

Just add 1 fresh chilli or 1 tsp dried chilli flakes and 1 level tsp of ground cumin.

BEETROOT AND ANISEED HOUMOUS

Add 1 large cooked beetroot (roughly chopped) and ½ level tsp aniseed seeds to the blender.

AUBERGINE ZAALOOK SALAD/DIP

I LOVE aubergines. I tried this in Morocco – it's a pretty classic recipe there, but
you can mix it up by adding your favourite spice. I sometimes omit the paprika and
add ground coriander instead. (See page 227 for photo)

SERVES 4

3 medium aubergines

3 large tomatoes,
  finely chopped

3 tbsp olive oil

a pinch of salt

¼ tsp freshly ground
  black pepper

¼ tsp red chilli pepper
  (optional)

1 heaped tsp paprika

1 tsp ground cumin

2 tbsp lemon juice
  or white wine vinegar

4 garlic cloves, crushed

8 tbsp flat-leaf parsley,
  finely chopped

crusty bread, to serve

Partially peel the aubergines and dice into very small cubes.

Drizzle the olive oil in a large pan, add the aubergine cubes
and salt to taste, then cover the pan and cook over a low heat
for 10 minutes. Using a spoon or potato masher, crush the
aubergine, then add the crushed tomatoes, garlic and spices
and mix well. Increase the heat, cover and cook for 15–20
minutes. Continue crushing and blending the aubergine and
tomato occasionally, until they are completely cooked and
have a smooth texture.

Mix the lemon juice or vinegar into the aubergine mixture and
simmer, uncovered, for 5 minutes, or until the liquid is reduced.
Adjust the seasoning, if necessary.

Sprinkle with parsley and serve warm or cold with crusty bread.

TAHINI DIP, TWO WAYS

Tahini is pulped sesame seeds. You can buy jars of it in most supermarkets
now – one jar goes a long way. (See page 227 for photo)

MAKES ENOUGH FOR 6–8

TAHINI DIP

2 heaped tbsp tahini
2–4 garlic cloves, crushed
½ tsp ground turmeric
juice of 2–3 lemons
1 tbsp olive oil, plus extra
    for drizzling
a pinch of salt,
chopped parsley,
    to garnish

Combine all the ingredients by beating hard (this can be done
in an electric blender, or with a balloon whisk if doing by hand).
Use the juice of 2 lemons first, then add more if necessary and
enough water to give a pouring consistency.

To serve, sprinkle with parsley and drizzle with olive oil.

YOGURT TAHINI DIP

1 heaped tbsp tahini
2 garlic cloves, crushed
a pinch of salt
1 tsp sumac
juice and zest of 2 lemons
50g (1 large tbsp)
    Greek yogurt

To serve

a pinch of paprika
lemon zest

Beat all the ingredients together, except for the juice of 1 lemon.
This dip should have more of a custardy consistency. Taste and
add the remaining lemon juice, if required.

To serve, sprinkle with a pinch of paprika and the lemon zest. It
also looks lovely with a few pomegranate seeds sprinkled on top.

AROMATIC LAMB CURRY

When I'm making this curry at home, the whole house smells delicious. Using lamb shanks makes it look so pretty and gives it dinner party status.

SERVES 4

3 tsp dried chilli flakes

2.5cm piece of ginger, grated

2 tsp cumin seeds

1 tsp black peppercorns

seeds from 5 cardamom pods

a pinch of salt

1 red onion, chopped

6 garlic cloves, crushed

1 lemongrass stalk, white part only, roughly chopped

2 tbsp coriander stems and leaves, chopped, plus a large handful of leaves, to serve

3 tbsp olive oil

4 lamb shanks (about 1.4kg)

400ml tin coconut milk

400ml water

1 tbsp caster sugar

1 tbsp fish sauce

400g new potatoes, halved

2 preserved lemons, sliced

1 tbsp lime juice

2 tbsp roasted peanuts, chopped

sourdough, to serve

Preheat the oven to 160°C/320°F/Gas Mark 3.

Combine the chilli flakes, ginger, cumin seeds, black peppercorns, cardamom and salt with the onion, garlic, lemongrass, coriander and 1 tbsp of the olive oil in a blender and blend as finely as possible.

Brown the lamb shanks in the remaining oil in a large flameproof casserole dish over a medium-high heat. Remove them from the pan and set aside, add the curry paste mixture and stir for 2 minutes.

Return the lamb to the dish, add the coconut milk, water, sugar and fish sauce and bring to the boil, then remove from the heat.

Add the potatoes and put in the oven for 1¾–2 hours, turning the lamb a few times while cooking, until the meat is tender and falling off the bone and the sauce has reduced by a third. Skim any fat off the surface and discard.

Stir in the preserved lemons and lime juice, and scatter with peanuts. Serve with coriander leaves and crusty sourdough bread.

SPICY CHOCOLATE POTS

These little chocolate mousses pack a powerful punch!

SERVES 4

120g dark chocolate
    (at least 80% cocoa
    solids), roughly
    chopped

1 tsp ground cinnamon

¼ tsp chilli flakes

a pinch of salt

3 tbsp strong spirit,
    such as Aqualibra
    tequila, Cointreau or
    Mastica liqueur

4 medium eggs, separated

40g soft brown sugar

zest of 1 orange

Put the chocolate into a heatproof glass bowl over a pan of simmering water, making sure the bowl does not touch the bottom of the pan, and melt gently. Remove the pan from the heat and stir in the cinnamon, chilli flakes and alcohol.

Beat the egg whites until they form peaks, then add the sugar and beat again until it turns glossy.

Stir the egg yolks into the cooled chocolate and then slowly fold in the egg whites, little by little. Do not overmix.

Spoon into small glasses, decorate with orange zest, and allow to set in the fridge for 2–3 hours.

RECIPES

FOR FERTILITY

CLOVES, FENNEL,
ANISEED

FIG AND FENNEL SALAD
AND BLUE CHEESE TOAST

I make this when I have friends coming round and we have lots of gossiping to do.
I just leave it on the table and we all dig in.

SERVES 4 AS A STARTER OR LIGHT MEAL

For the salad

2 small bulbs fennel, sliced
    thinly lengthways

1 tbsp olive oil

6 figs, halved

4 slices of prosciutto,
    torn (optional)

1 rosemary sprig,
    leaves picked and
    roughly chopped

2 tbsp snipped chives

2 tbsp red wine vinegar

1 tbsp honey

1 shallot, finely chopped

For the blue cheese toast

8 slices of sourdough

50g soft blue cheese,
    such as St Agur, Brie
    or any strong soft
    cheese you like

30g pecans, halved
    or chopped

Preheat a stovetop grill or pan over a high heat. Brush the fennel with 1 tsp of the olive oil and cook for 1–2 minutes on each side, or until lightly charred and just tender. Set aside to cool slightly.

Combine the fennel, figs, prosciutto (if using) rosemary and chives in a large bowl.

Whisk the remaining olive oil, vinegar, honey and shallot together in another bowl, add to the salad and toss gently.

Toast the bread slices, then spread with the blue cheese. Sprinkle the salad and toasts with the pecans, and serve.

JACKFRUIT AND MUSHROOM STIFADO

Stifado in Greek means to infuse or literally stuff with flavour, and that's exactly what this dish delivers. This is another of the dishes I made for The Real Greek restaurants, so if you like the sound of it and don't want to cook it you can pop in and try it there.

SERVES 6–8

3 large onions,
  finely chopped

2 garlic cloves, crushed

150ml olive oil

300g mushrooms,
  chopped

200g shallots

1 bay leaf

1 tsp aniseed

salt and freshly ground
  black pepper

90g tomato purée

400g tin chopped
  tomatoes,

540g tinned jackfruit

100ml water

500g vegetable stock

4 tbsp red wine vinegar

finely chopped parsley,
  to garnish

Soften the onion and garlic in the oil in a large pan on a low heat, for around 5 minutes. Add the mushrooms and shallots and fry until the juices begin to run. This should take 5–7 minutes. Add the spices and mix well. Add the tomato purée, mix and then add the chopped tomatoes.

Add the jackfruit, then pour in the water and stock and mix well. Check the seasoning.

Bring to the boil, then reduce the heat and simmer, uncovered, for 20–30 minutes, stirring occasionally. Add the vinegar and stir.

Remove from the heat and serve garnished with parsley.

GREEN BEANS, STEWED
WITH ONIONS, FENNEL AND TOMATOES

This mix of fennel and cinnamon can only be described as heavenly.

SERVES 4–6

100ml olive oil

300g onions, finely
chopped

4 garlic cloves, chopped

300g fennel bulb, sliced

350g chopped tomatoes
or cherry tomatoes

2 tsp ground cinnamon

salt and freshly ground
black pepper

400g green beans

chopped parsley,
to garnish

To serve

crusty bread

houmous (see page 225)

Gently heat the oil in a large saucepan over a low heat.
Add the chopped onions and sweat until opaque. Add
the garlic and stir well, then add the fennel and stir well.

Add the chopped tomatoes and cinnamon, and season
with salt and pepper. Simmer for 10 minutes,

Add the green beans and simmer for a further 10 minutes,
or until the beans are cooked but not soft.

Sprinkle the parsley on top and serve with a big chunk
of crusty bread and a dollop of houmous.

PECAN AND DATE SODA BREAD

I'm not the world's greatest baker, but even I can get this one right!

MAKES 1 LARGE LOAF

450g wholemeal rye flour
50g porridge oats
50g pecans, chopped
50g dried figs, chopped
50g pitted dried
  dates, chopped
1 tsp salt
1 tsp aniseed
1 tsp ground cinnamon
1 tsp ground mastic
1 tsp bicarbonate of soda
250ml buttermilk
200ml Greek yogurt
1 tbsp honey
butter, melted, for brushing

Preheat the oven to 180°C/350°F/Gas Mark 4 and line a baking sheet with baking paper.

Mix the flour, oats, pecans, figs, dates, salt, aniseed, cinnamon, mastic and bicarbonate of soda together in a large bowl.

Make a well in the middle of the mixture and pour in the buttermilk, yogurt and honey. Working quickly, mix everything together with your hands to form a sticky dough.

Turn the dough out onto the prepared baking sheet and form into a round. Use a sharp knife to mark the bread into quarters, cutting deeply, but not all the way through.

Place in the oven and cook for 50 minutes, or until a golden crust has formed. Remove from the oven and brush the top with the melted butter. Leave to cool on a wire rack.

CELERY SEED VINAIGRETTE
ON FENNEL AND LETTUCE SALAD

Celery seed has so many amazing health benefits – it helps support healthy
blood pressure and has great anti-inflammatory potential, so I couldn't resist
including this lovely dressing in the book.

SERVES 8

2 garlic cloves, crushed

salt and freshly ground
    black pepper

1½ tsp celery seeds,
    dry-toasted

3 tbsp raw apple
    cider vinegar

4 tbsp olive oil

4 tbsp sesame oil

2 heads green leaf lettuce,
    around 900g total, torn
    into small pieces

1 bulb fennel, thinly sliced

1 orange, sliced

First, make the vinaigrette. In a large bowl add the garlic, mix
sea salt and black pepper to taste, then add the celery seeds,
olive oil and sesame oil, vinegar and whisk together, blending
well. Taste and adjust the seasoning, if necessary.

Add the lettuce and fennel to the bowl, and toss to lightly coat
in the dressing. Add the orange segments and gently toss to
combine. Serve immediately.

SPICY SAUSAGE ROLLS

This is my version of the traditional British recipe, which is brimming with spice!

MAKES 8 LARGE OR 20 SMALL

3 tbsp olive oil

2 red onions, finely chopped

½ tsp ground cinnamon

1 tsp fennel seeds

2 tsp cumin seeds

1 carrot, finely diced

1 parsnip, coarsely grated

4 tbsp walnuts, chopped

4 tbsp of My Hot Spice Paste (see page 206) or harissa paste

4 garlic cloves, finely chopped

500g pork, lamb or turkey mince

4 tbsp flat-leaf parsley, chopped

zest and juice of 1 lemon

1 tsp salt

75g breadcrumbs

1 medium egg, plus 1 egg, beaten, for brushing

2 sheets of ready-rolled puff pasty

sesame and poppy seeds, for sprinkling

Preheat the oven to 190°C/375°F/Gas Mark 5 and line 2 baking trays with baking paper.

Heat the oil in a pan over a low heat, add the onions and spices and fry until the onions are soft and translucent. Add the carrot and parsnip and cook for a further 5–7 minutes.

Add the walnuts, Hot Spice Paste (or harissa paste) and garlic and mix well. Transfer the onion mixture to a bowl and use your hands to mix it with the mince, parsley, lemon zest and juice, salt and breadcrumbs. Add the egg and mix it into the mixture well.

Place the two sheets of pre-rolled puff pastry on a baking tray and cut both in half lengthways down the middle.

Divide the mince mixture into 4 portions, then make a long sausage along the middle of each piece of pastry. Brush the edges of the pastry with a little of the beaten egg and fold the pastry over the mince, pressing together firmly to seal.

Turn the rolls over so they are seam-side down on the baking tray and cut each of them into 4 pieces, making 16 in total.

Brush again with the beaten egg, then sprinkle with the sesame and poppy seeds. Bake in the oven for 25–30 minutes, or until the pastry is a lovely golden brown. Serve hot or cold.

FIG AND ORANGE MUFFINS

Figs are my favourite fruit and I love using them in sweet and savoury dishes. These spicy little muffins are wonderful for breakfast or with afternoon coffee.

MAKES 8

175g unsalted
  butter, softened

100g golden caster sugar

4 medium eggs, beaten

175g self-raising flour

zest and juice of 1 orange

½ tsp freshly ground
  black pepper

½ tsp ground cloves

1 tsp ground cinnamon

½ tsp ground turmeric

½ tsp ground mastic

200g fresh figs, stalks
  discarded, chopped,
  plus 1 whole fig for
  decoration (use fresh
  or dried if out of season)

100g walnut or pecan
  halves (optional)

70ml orange juice

2 tbsp honey

Preheat the oven to 180°C/350°F/Gas Mark 4. Line 8 holes of a deep muffin tin with paper or silicon muffin cases.

Using an electric whisk, beat the butter and sugar together in a large bowl until pale and fluffy. Add the eggs a little at a time, with 1 tbsp of the flour after each one, then fold in the remaining flour with the orange zest and spices until well mixed.

Add the chopped figs and nuts (if using) and mix gently until they are evenly distributed.

Spoon the muffin batter evenly into the muffin cases. Cut the remaining fig into thin wedges, then carefully place a wedge on top of each muffin. Bake in the oven for 35–40 minutes.

Meanwhile, warm the orange juice and honey together in a pan, then set aside until the muffins are golden and a skewer inserted in the centre comes out clean. Spoon the warm syrup over the muffins and leave to cool for 20 minutes in the tin, before transferring them to a wire rack to cool completely.

Note: Replace the figs with dried dates if you prefer.

RECIPES
TO BATTLE
FATIGUE

MINT, PARSLEY,
SUMAC

PIMM'S ICE LOLLIES

Beautifully refreshing on a hot sunny day.

MAKES ROUGHLY 6

500g strawberries, hulled

juice of 1 lemon

2 tbsp honey

12 mint leaves

9 tbsp Pimm's
(you can also use
pink gin if you like)

200ml lemonade

6cm piece of cucumber,
cut into ribbons

Put the strawberries in a food processor with the lemon juice, honey and half the mint leaves and blend to a smooth purée. Press through a fine sieve into a bowl, then stir in the Pimm's lemonade and the rest of the mint leaves. Set the mixture aside until the froth subsides.

Divide the mixture among ice-lolly moulds and add the cucumber ribbons and the rest of the mint leaves. Cover with a double-thickness sheet of foil (or the lids of the lolly moulds) and freeze for 2 hours, or until beginning to freeze. (If your moulds have covers with the stick in, just leave to freeze.)

After 2 hours, insert the lolly sticks, pushing them about halfway into the mixture, and return to the freezer for at least 8 hours, or until solid. Dip the moulds into hot water briefly, slide the lollies out and enjoy!

ONION, PEPPER, FETA AND POMEGRANATE TART

This dish is easy to throw together and so impressive on the table.

SERVES 6 AS A MAIN OR 12 AS A STARTER / MEZE

5 large onions, sliced

50g butter

4 tbsp olive oil

1 red pepper, sliced

1 yellow pepper, sliced

1 courgette, cut into ribbons

1 tbsp sumac

½ tsp ground turmeric

1 tsp freshly ground black pepper

1 tsp salt

200g cherry tomatoes

1 sheet of ready-rolled puff pastry (320g)

250g feta cheese

10 mint leaves, finely chopped

pomegranate molasses for drizzling

75g pomegranate seeds (optional)

1 tbsp brown sugar

2 green chillies, finely chopped (and de-seeded if you don't like too much heat)

Preheat the oven to 180°C/350°F/Gas Mark 4 and line a baking tray with baking paper.

Caramelise the onions in half the butter and oil in a pan over a medium heat for 10 minutes. Remove from the heat and place on a plate. Add the rest of the oil and butter to the pan, then add the peppers and sauté for a minute. Add the courgette, sumac, turmeric, black pepper and salt, and continue to cook for a further minute. Remove from the heat, add the tomatoes to the pan and roll them in the oil mixture.

Place the pre-rolled pastry on the prepared baking tray, rolling out a little more to go just over the edges, then fold them over to make a border.

Evenly spread the caramelised onions over the pastry, then add the pepper and tomato mix. Crumble the feta over the top and sprinkle with the mint leaves. Place in the oven for 20 minutes, or until the pastry has browned.

Remove from the oven, drizzle over the pomegranate molasses and sprinkle over the pomegranate seeds (if using). Serve immediately.

PORK DOLMADES, CYPRIOT-STYLE (KOUBEBPIA)

Apart from all the amazing spices in these dolmades, vine leaves are wonderful in themselves – there are many anti-ageing and heart health supplements made from them. Once you have made these, you can try using different fillings.

SERVES 6–8 AS A MAIN

about 50–60 vine leaves

2–3 tbsp olive oil

2 onions, finely chopped

½ bunch of parsley, finely chopped

½ small bunch of mint, chopped

1 tsp ground cinnamon

1kg coarsely ground pork mince

200g pudding rice

salt and freshly ground black pepper

400 g chopped tomatoes

1 lemon

Preheat the oven to 200°C/400°F/Gas Mark 6.

To prepare the vine leaves: if using fresh ones, blanch them in a bowl of hot water to soften. If using bottled leaves in brine, just rinse them.

Gently heat the olive oil in a saucepan, then add the onions and sweat them, but do not brown.

Add the parsley, mint and cinnamon, then add the meat and rice and season well. You are sealing the meat, not cooking it. Stir the mixture well, then remove from the heat.

Put the prepared vine leaves on plate. Destalk them and lay them down, with the smooth side on the outside. To roll, put 1 tsp of the meat mixture on the leaf, roll over and tuck both sides into the roll to make a little cigar shape. Put it into the ovenproof dish and continue until you have used up all the vine leaves and filling. Spread any remaining vine leaves on top like a blanket, then place an upside-down plate on top. Pour boiling water into your dish up to where it touches the plate.

Cover with foil and cook in the oven for 30 minutes, then lower the oven temperature to 180°C/350°F/Gas Mark 4 and cook for a further 30 minutes.

CRACKED WHEAT AND VEGETABLES

Being Cypriot, I use cracked wheat in many different ways, but this dish is brimming with vibrant deliciousness.

SERVES 6 AS A SIDE OR MEZE

60ml olive oil

2 medium onions, chopped

1 tsp ground cinnamon

1 tsp fresh sage, finely chopped

4 garlic cloves, finely chopped

2 medium carrots, diced

2 medium courgettes, diced

1 red pepper, diced

1 yellow pepper, diced

400g tin chopped tomatoes

salt and freshly ground black pepper

250g cracked wheat (bulgur)

300ml vegetable stock

To serve

½ bunch of parsley, chopped

drizzle of pomegranate molasses (optional)

seeds of 1 pomegranate (optional)

Gently heat the oil and soften the onions in a large saucepan pan on a low heat, without browning, then add the cinnamon and sage, then the garlic, carrots, courgettes and peppers and cook for 5 minutes. Add the tomatoes and season.

Add the cracked wheat and stir well for 1 minute, until it is coated with the vegetable mixture.

Add the vegetable stock, bring to the boil, then reduce the heat and simmer until all the liquid has been absorbed, stirring frequently to prevent the ingredients sticking to the base of the pan.

Serve with chopped parsley and a drizzle of pomegranate molasses and a sprinkling of pomegranate seeds, if you like.

SEABASS WRAPPED IN VINE LEAVES

Vine leaves are a wonderfood. Even though they are used here to seal the fish and hold the moisture in while cooking, you can eat them with the seabass, too.

SERVES 4

4 garlic cloves, peeled

1 tsp sumac

1 small bunch of parsley

1 small bunch of coriander

2.5cm piece of fresh ginger, peeled and roughly chopped

1 chilli

1 preserved lemon, deseeded

4 sea bass, scaled, gutted and washed

20 vine leaves (I use the ones from my garden, but you can use ones in brine)

olive oil, for brushing

a pinch of salt

Preheat the oven to 180°C/350°F/Gas Mark 4.

Place the garlic, sumac, parsley, coriander, ginger, chilli and preserved lemon in a blender and blitz to a chunky paste.

Divide the mixture into 4 portions and use to fill the fish cavities.

If using bottled vine leaves in brine, rinse them. If using fresh ones, blanch them in hot water for a few seconds to soften them.

Brush the fish with olive oil and wrap the vine leaves around them, vein-side in. Brush again with oil, season with sea salt and place on an baking tray lined with baking paper. Bake for 20 minutes – the skin should come away easily when it's ready. Serve immediately.

TOMATO SALAD

I like to make this when tomatoes are in season. We have a weekly food market in our area, and I buy my tomatoes from there, which come from the Isle of Wight. I love all the varieties and colours. Adding the nuts and fruit to this salad gives it some extra zing.

SERVES 6

1kg mixed tomatoes

1 tbsp sumac

a drizzle of good olive oil

a pinch of salt

½ small bunch of mint, finely sliced

1 quantity of tahini (see page 229) make this with extra lemon juice

Optional extras

100g walnut or pecan halves

100g golden berries or sour cherries

Cut all the tomatoes to similar-sized pieces. If using cherry tomatoes, cut them in half and cut the larger ones into similar-sized chunks. Place in a bowl, sprinkle with sumac, drizzle with a little olive oil and season with salt.

Sprinkle over the mint leaves and then drizzle with tahini. Add any of your chosen extras before serving.

RECIPES
TO REDUCE
STRESS

CARDAMOM,
THYME, OREGANO,
MARJORAM

CHAMOMILE AND THYME CUPCAKES

These soothing little cupcakes have an unusual flavour but they're the perfect afternoon treat.

MAKES 12

225g unsalted butter

160ml coconut milk

5 heaped tbsp dried chamomile flowers, plus extra to decorate

100g caster sugar

3 medium eggs

1 tsp thyme leaves, plus small sprigs to decorate

210g plain wholemeal spelt flour

1½ tsp baking powder

a pinch of salt

100g icing sugar

Preheat the oven to 180°C/350°F/Gas mark 4. Line a 12-hole muffin tin with paper cases.

Heat the butter, coconut milk and chamomile flowers in a small pan over a low heat until the butter has completely melted, then simmer for a few minutes. Remove from the heat and allow to cool for 5 minutes.

Once cooled, strain the tea, collecting the chamomile-infused liquid in a bowl and discarding the flowers. There should be around 250ml of liquid remaining.

Divide the liquid into two bowls, one containing two thirds of the liquid and the other containing the remaining third to use for the icing. Place the bowls in the fridge for 20 minutes until the butter has set slightly.

Beat the larger portion of the mixture with the sugar. Add the eggs and the thyme leaves, then slowly fold in the flour, baking powder and salt until combined. Add a dash more coconut milk if the mixture is too thick. Divide the batter between the paper cases and bake in the oven for 15–20 minutes.

For the icing, beat the remaining chamomile-infused butter, gradually adding the icing sugar until thick. Chill in the fridge while the cupcakes are cooling.

Top each cupcake with as much icing as you like, then decorate with a single chamomile flower and a small thyme sprig.

CHICKEN TAGINE
WITH PRESERVED LEMONS AND OLIVES

I'm obsessed with preserved lemons – they add incredible zing to stews like this one.

SERVES 2

1 preserved lemon

50ml olive oil

1 tsp melted butter

2 garlic cloves,
    finely chopped

2.5cm piece of
    ginger, grated

1 tbsp ground coriander

a pinch of saffron strands

1 cinnamon stick

500g whole chicken,
    cut into large chunks

1 red onion, finely
    chopped

salt and freshly ground
    black pepper

10 green olives

2 tbsp parsley,
    finely chopped

1 small bunch of
    coriander, roughly
    chopped

1 tbsp marjoram, finely
    chopped

couscous or crusty bread,
    to serve

Cut the preserved lemon in half and separate the flesh from the peel. Set the peel aside and finely chop the flesh.

Place the chopped lemon flesh in a casserole dish. Add the olive oil, melted butter, garlic, ginger, ground coriander, saffron, cinnamon stick and 250ml cold water and mix well.

Add the chicken pieces to the casserole, having pierced them with a sharp knife so they absorb the spices. Mix all the ingredients together until the chicken pieces are coated in the marinade. Add the chopped onion and mix well.

Cover the casserole with a lid and sear the chicken pieces over a low heat for 15 minutes. Keep the lid on to keep the moisture in. Turn each piece of chicken over and add a little water, if necessary.

After 10 minutes, add 250ml cold water. Increase the heat to medium, cover and bring to the boil. Cook, covered, for 30 minutes, checking the chicken occasionally and adding water if necessary. There should always be enough sauce at the bottom of the tagine so the meat doesn't burn.

Season, add the lemon peel and olives to the tagine and continue cooking, uncovered, for a few minutes, until the sauce slightly thickens.

Sprinkle with chopped herbs and black pepper, and serve hot with couscous or crusty bread.

MARINATED PORK CHOPS
WITH EDAMAME MASH

This is a jazzed up version of a simple pork recipe, with some lovely oriental elements.

SERVES 4

4 pork chops, about
    140g each

2 tsp sesame oil

2 chillies, chopped
    (optional)

For the marinade

2 tbsp oregano
    leaves, chopped

3 tbsp thyme sprigs

1 tsp fennel seeds, crushed

1 tbsp salt

2 garlic cloves

zest and juice of 1 orange

zest and juice of 2 limes

½ tsp caster sugar

For the edamame mash

200g frozen
    edamame beans

250g frozen peas

1 tbsp olive oil

1 red onion, finely
    chopped

2 chillies, chopped

1 thumb-sized piece
    of ginger, grated

½ bunch of mint, finely

50g Greek yogurt

zest and juice of 1 lime

salt and freshly ground
    black pepper

Mix all the marinade ingredients together in a bowl large enough to hold the pork chops. Add the chops and rub well with the marinade. Cover and leave for 4 hours, or overnight.

Bring a large pan of water to the boil. Add the edamame beans and cook for 4 minutes, then add the peas and cook for a further 2 minutes. Drain in a sieve and set aside.

Return the pan to the heat, add the olive oil, onion, chillies and ginger and cook for 4–5 minutes.

Tip the edamame beans and peas back into the pan and roughly mash with a potato masher. Turn off the heat and stir in the mint, yogurt and lime zest and juice, then season to taste. Cover to keep warm.

Heat a stovetop griddle pan until hot.

Drizzle the chops with the sesame oil and cook on the griddle pan for 5 minutes on each side, or until cooked through. Remove from the pan, cover with foil and allow to rest.

Serve the chops on top of the edamame mash, sprinkled with chilli.

BAKED WHITE CABBAGE
WITH ORANGE, CARDAMOM AND HONEY

This recipe celebrates the underrated cabbage in all its glory.

SERVES 4

8 green cardamom pods

1 large white cabbage

3 tbsp extra-virgin olive oil

125ml orange juice

35ml white wine

100ml chicken or
    vegetable stock

1 tbsp honey

a generous pinch of
    chilli flakes

½ tsp coriander seeds,
    crushed

salt and freshly ground
    black pepper

Preheat the oven to 190°C/375°F/Gas Mark 5.

Crush the cardamom pods until they break open. Tip the seeds inside into a mortar and pestle and grind them as finely as you can. Slice the cabbage into wedges.

Heat the oil in a large ovenproof frying pan. Fry the cabbage wedges over a high heat on both sides so they get a good golden brown colour. You may have to do this in batches. Once all the wedges are browned, put them all back into the pan.

Add all the remaining ingredients with some seasoning and cook in the oven for about 30–40 minutes, turning the pieces of cabbage over occasionally, until tender and you have a little juice left in the base of the pan. Serve.

POT-ROAST CHICKEN
WITH RED WINE AND WILD MUSHROOMS

This succulent and moist chicken stew is a really simple and delicious dish.

SERVES 4

1.6kg free-range
    organic chicken

olive oil

salt and freshly ground
    black pepper

150ml red wine

150ml chicken stock

8 garlic cloves, peeled

1 bay leaf

300–400g mixed
    mushrooms, such as
    chestnut, oyster and
    shiitake, chopped

25g unsalted butter

1 tsp fresh oregano

50g crème fraîche

2 tsp fresh oregano,
    for sprinkling

Preheat the oven to 180°C/350°F/Gas Mark 4. Have a large lidded casserole, at least 2.5 litres capacity, ready.

Heat a medium frying pan over a high heat. Using your hands, lightly coat the chicken with oil. Season with salt and pepper, then add the chicken to the pan and brown it on all sides. Place the chicken, breast-side up, in the casserole.

Add the red wine, stock, garlic and bay leaf to the casserole. Bring the liquid to the boil, cover with the lid and cook in the oven for 1 hour.

About 10 minutes before the chicken is cooked, heat a knob of butter with 1 tsp olive oil in a large frying pan over a medium heat. Add the mushrooms and oregano and season with salt and pepper. Fry for 3–5 minutes, stirring frequently, until golden and any liquid has evaporated.

Remove the chicken from the casserole, tipping any juices from inside it back into the pot, and set aside on a warm plate to rest for 15–20 minutes. Discard the bay leaf and skim off any fat on the surface. Add the mushrooms to the casserole and simmer for a few minutes.

Ladle one-third of the mushrooms and a little of the cooking liquor into a liquidiser and purée, then stir back into the casserole. Add the crème fraîche and gently reheat.

Carve the chicken and serve with the mushroom sauce and a sprinkling of oregano.

REVANI GREEK SEMOLINA CAKE

This cake transports me straight back to my grandmother's kitchen.

SERVES 8–10

150g coconut oil, plus
    extra for greasing

250g semolina

100g caster sugar

100g ground almonds

3 tsp baking powder

1 large unwaxed orange

3 medium eggs

**For the honey and
    orange syrup**

100ml honey

zest and juice of 1 lemon

2 cloves

1 cinnamon stick

4 thyme sprigs

To decorate (optional)

3 tsp pistachios,
    finely chopped

2 tsp rose petal jam or
    orange marmalade

1 tsp lemon juice

Preheat the oven to 200°C/400°F/Gas Mark 6. Line the base of a 24cm loose-bottomed round cake tin with baking paper, then grease with coconut oil.

Mix the semolina, sugar, almonds and baking powder together in a bowl.

Cut the orange into small pieces, removing any pips, then put in a blender and blitz to a pulp.

Whisk the oil with the eggs in another bowl, then add to the dry ingredients and mix well. Fold in the orange pulp, then pour the mixture into the prepared tin. Bake in the oven for 10 minutes. Reduce the oven temperature to 180°C/350°F/Gas Mark 4 and bake for a further 20–25 minutes until a skewer inserted into the middle of the cake comes out clean. Cover with foil if the top is getting too brown. Allow to cool in the tin for 15 minutes before turning out onto a plate.

To make the spiced syrup, put all the ingredients, including 5 tbsp water, into a saucepan and bring gently to the boil, stirring until the honey has completely dissolved. Reduce the heat and simmer for 10 minutes, remove from the heat and allow to cool.

While the cake is still hot, pierce it several times with a skewer, then spoon the syrup all over the cake, allowing it to run into the holes. If any excess syrup starts to seep out from around the cake, scoop it up with a spoon and pour over again until everything is soaked up. Sprinkle the pistachios on top and allow to cool completely.

Eat like this or serve with rose yogurt made by mixing 200g Greek yogurt, 2 heaped tbsp icing sugar and 4 tbsp rose water.

CHERRY AND GINGER BANANA LOAF

This is the perfect tea-time cake – the dried cherries add that little bit of tartness for an afternoon pick-me-up.

SERVES 8–12

140g unsalted butter,
melted, plus extra
for greasing

270g plain wholemeal
rye flour, plus extra
for dusting

1 Earl Grey tea bag

250ml boiling water

100g dried cherries

100g light brown
soft sugar

3 ripe bananas, mashed
plus 1 to decorate

2 medium eggs

1 tsp baking powder

2 tsp ground cinnamon

1 tsp ground ginger

5 cardamom seeds,
shelled and crushed

zest and juice of 1 orange

Preheat the oven to 160°C/325°F/Gas Mark 3. Lightly grease a 900g loaf tin, then line the base with baking paper and lightly dust the sides with a little flour.

Place the tea bag in a mug with the boiling water, add the cherries and allow to soak in the tea for 10 minutes.

Beat the sugar and eggs together with a fork. Add the mashed bananas and mix together until it looks like cake batter. Then add the flour, baking powder, cinnamon, ginger and cardamom seeds and mix thoroughly to combine.

Pour in the melted butter and beat until it is mixed in. Drain the cherries and add them to the mixture, together with the orange juice and zest.

Pour the cake mixture into the prepared tin and level the top. Cut the last banana into slices lengthways and lay on the cake.

Bake in the oven for 1 hour 20 minutes until firm and a skewer inserted into the centre comes out clean. Remove the loaf from the tin and allow it to cool on a wire rack before serving.

PITTAKIA

This way of cooking was originally developed by the Greek settlers, who in the fifth century BC founded Neapolis (New Town, Italy). They adapted a pre-existing baking tradition to develop this new 'pita', which through experimentation, luck and linguistic distortion, became pizza. It ALL started with the Greeks!

MAKES 2 PITTAKIA, EACH SERVING 2–3

450g white or brown bread flour, plus extra for dusting

½ tsp dried thyme

½ tsp dried oregano

½ tsp dried basil

1 tsp salt

7g sachet fast-action dried yeast

½ tsp caster sugar

280ml lukewarm water

1 tbsp olive oil, plus extra for coating

For the topping

250ml crème fraîche

2 medium red onions, finely sliced

150–200g combined weight of the following:

crumbled feta/pitted Kalamata olives/

roasted artichokes/ sundried tomatoes, sliced/oregano/

chestnut mushrooms/ hiromeri/

capers/anchovies

freshly ground black pepper

Mix the flour, herbs, salt, yeast and sugar together in a large bowl. Stir in the water and oil and mix together to form a soft (but not sticky) dough.

Turn the dough out onto a lightly floured work surface and knead well for 10 minutes. Return the dough to the bowl and coat with a little oil. Cover with cling film and leave at room temperature until it has doubled in size.

Preheat the oven to 230°C/450°F/Gas Mark 8. Prepare the topping of your choice. Knock back the risen dough, then turn it out onto a lightly floured work surface and divide it into 2 equal portions. Roll one portion out into a very thin rectangle, about the same size as your baking tray. Don't worry if the dough stretches or overlaps the edges, as they can be folded in at a later stage. Repeat with the second piece of dough on the second baking tray.

Spread one sheet of dough with half the crème fraîche, then sprinkle on half the onion slices and half your toppings. Season with black pepper to taste. Fold over the edges to make a narrow border of about 1cm.

Repeat with the second sheet of dough. Bake for 12–15 minutes until golden and crisp. Eat immediately.

SUGAR-FREE CARDAMOM, PECAN AND PARSNIP LOAF

I often put veg into cakes and muffins because they add moisture and nutrients, too.
If you don't like parsnips, use grated carrot or courgette instead.

SERVES 8–10

100g pecan halves

150ml coconut oil

3 medium eggs

170g wholemeal flour

2 tsp baking powder

½ tsp salt

½ tsp allspice

1 tsp green cardamom pods, seeds removed and crushed in pestle and mortar

150g dried pitted dates, chopped

200g parsnip, grated

For the honey frosting

180g soft cheese

1 tbsp honey, plus extra to drizzle (optional)

zest and juice of 1 small lemon

a pinch of salt

Preheat the oven to 170°C/325°F/Gas Mark 3. Line a 900g loaf tin with baking paper.

Spread the pecan halves on a baking tray and toast them in the oven for 10–12 minutes, keeping an eye on them so that they don't burn. When they're nicely toasted, take them out, allow them to cool and then chop into small pieces.

Whisk the oil and eggs together with a fork. Fold in the flour, baking powder, salt, spices and dates. Fold in the parsnip and most of the pecans, reserving some for decoration. Pour the mixture into the prepared tin and bake in the oven for 1 hour, or until risen and golden.

For the frosting, beat the cheese with a fork until softened, then stir in the honey, lemon zest and juice and salt. Spread the frosting over the top of the cake and top with the remaining pecans and a drizzle of honey before serving.

ORANGE, CARDAMOM AND ALMOND CAKE

When I bake this cake, the kitchen fills with the warming smell of cardamom.
I serve it on its own or with Greek yogurt that I have mixed with icing sugar and
rosewater to make it even more aromatic.

SERVES 12

zest and juice of
   2 large oranges

250g dried pitted
   dates, chopped

200g butter, softened

150g light
   muscovado sugar

4 medium eggs

250g spelt flour

1 tsp baking powder

seeds from 10 cardamom
   pods, crushed

100g ground almonds

50g pistachio
   nuts, bashed

a pinch of salt

1 small orange, finely
   sliced, to decorate

4 tbsp icing sugar

Preheat the oven to 140°C/275°F/Gas Mark 1. Line the base
of a 21cm loose-bottomed cake tin with baking paper.

Set aside 2 tbsp of the orange juice and a little of the zest, then
place the rest in a small saucepan with the dates and heat for
3 minutes. Remove from the heat and allow to cool.

Using an electric whisk, beat the butter and light muscovado
sugar together in a bowl for 3 minutes until pale and creamy.
Beat in the eggs one at a time, adding 1 tbsp of the flour to
stop it from curdling. Fold in the remaining flour, the baking
powder, cardamom seeds, ground almonds, pistachios and
a pinch of salt.

Stir in the cooled dates and juice mixture, then spoon the
mixture into the prepared tin. Level the surface and decoratively
lay the orange slices on the surface of the cake mixture. Bake
for 1 hour 50 minutes–2 hours or until a knife inserted into the
centre comes out clean. Cover with foil if the top of the cake is
browning too much during cooking. Allow to cool in the tin for
30 minutes, then remove and cool on a wire rack.

When the cake has cooled completely, mix the reserved
orange juice and zest and the icing sugar together to make
an icing. Drizzle over the cake and serve.

RECIPES
FOR LOSING
WEIGHT

CINNAMON, GARLIC,
ALLSPICE

APPLE STRUDEL

When I bake this for my family, they think Christmas has come early. The aromatic mix of clove and cinnamon that wafts through the kitchen is amazing.

SERVES 4–6

150g butter, either salted or unsalted

75g caster sugar

25g demerara sugar

3 Bramley apples, peeled, cored and sliced

6 Cox apples or other eating apples, peeled, cored and diced

8 dates, roughly chopped

30g sultanas

½ tsp ground cloves

2 tsp ground cinnamon

6 large sheets of filo pastry

4 tbsp pecans, chopped

hot custard, to serve

Place 75g of the butter and the caster sugar into a heavy-based pan and heat until the butter is foaming and the sugar is beginning to melt. Add the Bramley apples and cook for a few minutes until tender.

Stir in the Cox apples, dates, sultanas, cloves and 1 tsp of the cinnamon and continue to cook until the apples are just cooked and beginning to soften.

Transfer the apple mixture to a dish and either allow to cool at room temperature or place in the fridge.

Preheat the oven 190°C/375°F/Gas Mark 5 and line a baking tray with baking paper.

Once the filling is cool, begin to layer up the strudel. Melt the remaining butter in a pan, then lay a sheet of filo on the prepared tray and brush with a little of the butter. Place the next sheet on top and brush with more butter, repeating until all the sheets are buttered and layered.

Spoon the filling along the length of the pastry and roll the pastry around the filling to form a long parcel, tucking in the ends as you go. Brush the top of the strudel with any remaining butter and sprinkle with the demerara sugar and half the remaining cinnamon.

Bake in the oven for 30 minutes, then sprinkle with the pecans.

Return to the oven for 10 minutes until golden. Allow to cool for 5 minutes, then sprinkle with the last of the cinnamon. Serve in slices with hot custard.

LENTIL AND COCONUT CURRY
WITH MINI PORK MEATBALLS

Is this a stew or a soup? I'm not sure, but with all these aromatic spices in it,
one thing is for sure – it's delicious!

SERVES 4

2 tsp coriander seeds

1 tbsp olive oil

2 large celery sticks,
    finely chopped

6 garlic cloves, crushed

2 small red chillies,
    thinly sliced, plus
    extra to serve

250g split red lentils

400ml reduced-fat
    coconut milk

1 litre fresh chicken stock

salt and freshly ground
    black pepper

400g pork mince

40g mint leaves, finely
    chopped

4 tsp fish sauce

2 limes

Toast the coriander seeds in a large pan over a low heat
for about 4 minutes until fragrant, then lightly crush in a pestle
and mortar. Tip onto a plate and set aside.

Heat the oil in the pan over a medium heat. Add the celery,
garlic and chillies and cook for 5 minutes. Stir in the toasted
seeds and lentils and cook for a further 2 minutes. Add the
coconut milk, stock and 100ml water, then season and bring
to the boil. Reduce the heat and simmer for 25 minutes, or
until the lentils are tender.

Meanwhile, mix the pork mince with half the chopped mint
and fish sauce and shape into 20 meatballs, about 2 tsp each,
then chill for 20 minutes.

Lower the meatballs gently into a frying pan over a medium-
high heat and turn every few minutes until their outsides are
brown and slightly crisp.

Add the meatballs to the lentil mixture and simmer for 10 minutes,
turning halfway through cooking. Add the juice of one of the limes
and stir through.

Serve topped with the remaining mint, extra chilli and fish sauce
with the extra lime on the side.

FIG AND ALMOND CAKE
WITH ORANGE BLOSSOM YOGURT

When they are in season I use fresh figs, but if they're not I use the soft organic ones instead.

SERVES 10

200g unsalted butter
   at room temperature

75g brown sugar

3 medium eggs

180g ground almonds

100g wholemeal flour

½ tsp salt

1 vanilla pod, split in half
   and seeds scraped out

1 tsp ground cinnamon

100g Greek yogurt

4 tsp ground cloves

a pinch of saffron
   threads (optional)

12 figs

**For the orange
blossom yogurt**

100g Greek yogurt

25g icing sugar or
   1 tbsp honey

4–5 tbsp orange
   blossom water

Preheat the oven to 200°C/400°F/Gas Mark 6. Line the base and sides of a 24cm loose-bottomed cake tin with baking paper.

Beat the butter and sugar together with a hand-held electric mixer until pale and fluffy.

Beat each egg separately, then, with the machine on medium speed, add them one at a time to the bowl, adding another only once the previous egg is fully combined.

Mix the almonds, flour, salt, vanilla seeds, saffron threads and cinnamon together in a bowl, then fold into the cake mixture. Mix until smooth, then fold in the yogurt.

Pour the cake mixture into the prepared tin and level roughly with a palette knife or a spoon.

Cut each fig vertically into four wedges and arrange in circles on top of the cake, just slightly immersed in the cake mixture.

Bake in the oven for 15 minutes, then reduce the temperature to 170°C/325°F/Gas Mark 3 and continue baking for 60 minutes, or until it's firm to the touch. Cover with foil if it starts to brown too quickly on top.

Remove the cake from the oven and allow it to cool in the tin.

To serve, mix all the orange blossom yogurt ingredients together in a bowl and serve it with the cake.

BERRY AND COCONUT
ICE LOLLIES

These are a perfect refreshing summer treat.

MAKES 8

280g mixed strawberries, raspberries and blueberries (fresh or frozen)

400ml tin coconut milk

2 tbsp honey, plus extra to taste

a pinch of ground cinnamon

Hull the strawberries (if using fresh) and put in a blender with the other berries. Add the coconut milk, cinnamon and honey, adding more to taste, and blend until smooth.

Divide the mixture between eight 150ml lolly moulds and secure an upright lolly stick in each. Freeze for at least 4 hours, until completely solid.

Dip the outside of the moulds in hot water for a few seconds to release, and serve.

TURMERIC LATTE

If you really want to make a difference to your aches, pains and
general health, drink one of these every day.

SERVES 2

3cm piece of fresh
  turmeric, peeled or ¾
  tsp ground turmeric

2cm piece of fresh ginger,
  peeled or ¼–½ tsp
  ground ginger·

1 tsp honey

1 tbsp almond, cashew
  or hazelnut butter

350ml water, or milk,
  hazelnut milk or oat milk
  for a creamier drink

½–¾ tsp ground
  cinnamon, plus extra
  to serve

1 tsp vanilla extract

salt and freshly ground
  black pepper

Place all the ingredients in a blender and blend until smooth
and frothy. Then transfer to a small saucepan and heat gently
until warm.

Pour into mugs, sprinkle over more cinnamon and serve.

ACKNOWLEDGEMENTS

I've had such a lovely team working on this book and there are so many people to thank!

First is Kyprianos Constantinou, without whom this book would not have been written. He is a wonderful nutritionist and health psychologist with a brilliant brain, and he writes beautifully and is so knowledgeable. If you ever get the chance to go to any of his talks, you should – they are so enlightening.

Thank you, as always, to my colleagues at The Real Greek: Emily, Christos, Viola and Monika, and of course the big Boss Nabil. I love working with you all, and thank you for letting me use The Real Greek as my office.

Thank you to all the team at Blink, including the gorgeous duo of Lisa Hoare and Karen Browning, who make writing a pleasure and are always so supportive and generally wonderful, and such hotties too. Thanks also to Natalie Jerome and Kate Murrant at Lagom.

A huge thank you to Carly Cook, who is the most excellent project manager, and such a brilliant editor that she makes me sound good! Carly, you are such a joy to work with – I only want to make books with you. Thank you also for putting together the BEST TEAM for our shoot. Abi Hartshorne, my art director and designer, you have made my book a beauty. Andrew Burton, your pictures actually have smell-o-vision as they look so tasty and vibrant; and thank you to Lisa Paige-Smith, your lovely assistant. Hannah Wilkinson your props were divine, thank you!

Thank you so much to Jaswinder Jhalli and Gahz Ahmad, not only wonderful food stylists but such lovely, kind people and just a joy to work with. Thank you, Jas, for your recipe tweaking, to make them just right.

Get the trumpets out and sound the salute . . . Thank you Princess no, *Queen Vickie*, my manager at White Management. She can be so pushy and gets me to do things I think I don't want to do, but then, once I've done them, I am so happy. You are my wonderful, supportive friend and I thank you for that.

Thank you to my children, Antigoni, Sophia, Zephyros and Zeno. I can't wait to see what amazing things you do with your lives, though if you decide you don't want to do anything and just live with me forever, I'm good with that, too. I love you all very much.

As always, my biggest thanks go to my husband. Without him I would have nothing. He is the one who pushes me, supports me and makes me so much better than I am. I love you Paul.